KILN-FIRED GLASS

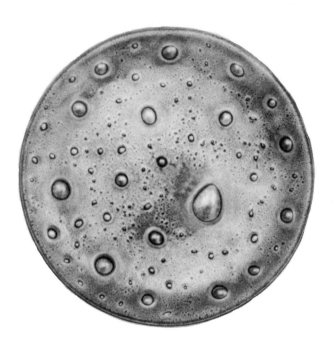

KILN-FIRED GLASS

HARRIETTE ANDERSON

CHILTON BOOK COMPANY

Radnor, Pennsylvania

Color Illustrations, Front Panel: *(Top)* "Plate" by Michael and Frances Higgins; *(Left)* "Tree Platter" by Michael and Frances Higgins; *(Bottom)* "A Happening" by Harriette Anderson. Back Panel: *(Top)* "Bowl" by Michael and Frances Higgins; *(Left)* "Water Lily" by Harriette Anderson; *(Right)* A Panel by Harriette Anderson.

Published in Radnor, Pa., by Chilton Book Company and simultaneously in Don Mills, Ontario, Canada, by Thomas Nelson & Sons, Ltd.

ISBN   0-8019-5540-8
Library of Congress Catalog Card Number 77-116917

Designed by William E. Lickfield

Manufactured in the United States of America

To my husband whose many breakfasts included a look at the glass that had cooled in the night.

A Statement

Glass objects have been found that date back into B.C. Through the ages, the use of glass has increased until now it plays a major part as a utilitarian material and as an art form.

Until recently, glass, whether produced for practical use or as an object of art, was started in a molten stage. First the liquid was poured into a mold or blown by the use of a blowpipe. Then, depending upon the plan to enhance it further, it was passed along for additional decorating with glazes or by engraving. Sheet glass was rolled, using several methods, or blown.

Glazes have been applied for many centuries to opaque backgrounds such as china and pottery. Their use has become a highly developed medium, which craftsmen have further explored and improved upon in the twentieth century, with evidence of great progress.

In 1947, intrigued by the possibilities of sagging or bending glass, a process that for years had been used in making curved windshields, Maurice Heaton, Frances and Michael Higgins, Earl McCutchen and others concentrated on developing methods that combine gilding, enameling, and laminating, often sandwiching other substances between layers of glass.

At first, their forms were limited to shallow bowls, plates, and plaques and their main efforts were concentrated on developing adequate mold substances, on gaining familiarity with the properties of commercially available plate and window glass, and on studying the reaction of these glasses to the substances that were either applied to the surface or fused between the layers when fired in a kiln.

A new craft was born, without the use of large furnaces and other elaborate equipment. An art medium was developed which enabled the craftsman to work with glass in the home using easily accessible materials and equipment.

In this book, the characteristics of glass have been retained and the designing has become a part of the glass.

The information written on the following pages is a tool. It offers a starting place, with the hope that the craftsman will find it only that, with the excitement for exploring beyond.

HARRIETTE ANDERSON

Acknowledgments

Many people become involved when a craftsman undertakes to share, in the form of a book, what he has learned about his craft. The photographers, friends, and fellow craftsmen are all important parts of the whole.

My special thanks go to Mr. Walter Rinne, Chief of the Projects Division of the United States Department of the Interior, whose hobby is photography. Mr. Rinne is responsible for all of the step-by-step pictures and some of the fired pieces. His ability as a photographer is surpassed only by his unlimited patience.

Mrs. Hazel Marsh assisted in the first rewriting of some of the chapters. Her time-consuming guidance proved invaluable for later writing. This is to express a deep appreciation for her efforts.

Mr. Given W. Cleek, Research Chemist of the Inorganic Glass Section at the National Bureau of Standards, compared pieces of glass fired under different conditions to determine the degree of annealing achieved. His direction in the study of annealing glass was most helpful.

Mr. John Warwick of the Miles Glass Company in Arlington, Virginia, secured glass as it was needed, sometimes on very short notice. I am grateful to him for his cooperation.

My thanks go also to the craftsmen and organizations who provided examples of their work:

Bette Bartelmes, a student at the University of Michigan in the School of Graduate Studies.

Mr. Richard B. Beaman, an associate professor of art at Carnegie Mellon University in Pittsburgh, Pennsylvania. His glass installations are at Wayne University and many other places. He is an accomplished oil painter.

Mariette Bevington, whose formal education includes a three year diploma course in Mural Design and Painting and two years of study of Stained Glass Design and Techniques at the Central School of Art and Design in London, England. She received the Tiffany Award for Stained Glass Design in 1962-63. Her work may be seen in many churches and other buildings.

John B. Buescher, who designed and executed the glued stained glass panel, is a student at the University of Virginia.

Michael and Frances Higgins, a husband and wife team, have been well known over a long period of time for their outstanding work. They helped in the development of many glass techniques.

Earl McCutchen, instructor, potter, craftsman in glass and head of his department at the University of Georgia. His educational television series on pottery included a program on glass.

Joy McFarland, an oil painter who has received acclaim for her work using the technique of the old masters, has recently turned to stitchery in addition to painting.

Ruth Walters, who with her husband Stan, devotes her efforts to pottery on a full-time basis. Together their outstanding work as potters has won them recognition in many shows. Their sought-after pieces may be found in some of the country's best shops.

Blenko Glass Company provided pictures showing how a sheet of glass is blown. Their visitors' center is most interesting.

Bohemia Glass Company, Prague, Czechoslovakia

American Swedish News Exchange, New York, New York

The Finnish Embassy, Washington, D.C.

Royal Leerdam Glass Works, Leerdam, The Netherlands

Contents

A Statement   vi

Acknowledgments   ix

1. WORKING WITH   The Glass Blank   1
   GLASS   1   Preparation   1
                           Selecting the Glass   1
                           To Clean Glass   3
                           Blanks in Relation to the Mold   3

2. EQUIPMENT   4   Kilns   4
                           Ceramic   4
                           Large Enameling Kilns   5
                           Small Enameling Kilns   5
                        The Kiln Shelf   6
                        Firebrick Posts   8
                        Pyrometers   8
                        Pyrometric Cones   9
                        Sifters   9
                        Tools   10
                        Electric Sprayers   12

3. MATERIALS AND HOW   Colorants   14
   TO USE THEM   14   Glass Colors—Liquids   14
                           Powdered Glass   14
                           Opaque Enamel Powders   15
                           Embossed Pieces, Opaque   15
                           Embossed Pieces, Ices   16
                           Embossed Pieces—Transparent and
                             Some Opaque Enamels   16
                           Other Glass Decorating Powders 16
                           Painting Materials—Opaque   17

                                                           xi

		Applying a Design with Oil	17
		Slip Trailing with Glazes	18
		Color Samples	20
		Other Materials	22
		Use of a Sprayer	23
		Clear Flux on Top of Glass	25
		Bases for Mixing Enamels	25
4. MOLDS	27	Greenware	27
		Wax Impressions for Clay Molds	29
		Clay Pinchpots	31
		Carved Firebrick	33
		Use of the Outside of a Mold	35
		Preparing the Mold	36
		Designing with a Separator	37
5. CUTTING GLASS	38	Using a Straight Glass Cutter	38
		Cutting Circles	46
		To Correct Rough Edges	48
		Position of the Cutter	48
		Breaking Up a Bottle	50
6. TECHNIQUES FOR LAMINATING AND DECORATING GLASS	51	Lamination	51
		Compatibility of Glasses	51
		Applying the Design with Oil	53
		One Color on One Blank	54
		Two Colors on One Blank	55
		Two Colors on Two Blanks	59
		Removing the Oil	64
		Uses of Transparent Powders for Backgrounds	64
		Assembly Before Firing	65
		Sgraffito	65
		Dry Powder	65
		Coating of Oil on a Blank	70
		The Combination of Embossing and Sgraffito	70

Designing with Bubbles	73
Single Bubbles	73
Doubling the Bubbles	76
Random Bubbles	77
Unplanned Bubbles	81
Embossed Designs on Plate Glass	81
The Design on the Underside	82
Plate Glass	82
Laminated Single- and Double-	
strength Glass	84
Three Blanks	88
Embossed Panels	89
A Happening	89
Transparent Plate Glass with Color	89
7. SILK SCREEN PRINTING ON GLASS 92		
Making a Screen	93
Applying the Design	96
Using a Liquid	96
Using the Blockout	97
Preparing for Printing	99
Preparing the Colorant	100
Mixing	101
Printing the Design	101
Cleaning the Screen	103
Printing Two Colors on One Blank	103
Printing Two Colors on Two Blanks	104
Paper Technique	105
Applying the Design with Glue	108
Silk Screen Kits	111
How to Make a Decal	111
Procedure	111
Transfer Printing	114
Block	114
Silk Screen	116

8. FIRING SCHEDULES	117	Know Your Kiln	117
		Test Fire	118
		Ventilating the Kiln	119
		Top-loading Kilns	119
		Front-loading Kilns	119
		Firing	119
		Firing Flat	120
		Firing on Molds	120
		Reasons Behind the Firing Schedule	121
		A Simplified Schedule	123
		Firing Schedule for Laminated Single- and Double-strength Glass and Plate Glass	123
		Single Blanks	124
		Firing Schedule for Antique Glass	125
		Two Firings	125
		Laminated	125
		Single Blanks	126
9. ANNEALING OF GLASS	127	Annealing without a Pyrometer	130
		Annealing Stained Glass	130
		Preannealing	131
		Conclusion	132
10. STAINED GLASS	134	About Stained Glass	134
		Fusing	134
		Slumped Blank with the Design Embossed	137
		Curved Pieces for Water-Lily	137
		Pieces Fired Flat	139
		Non-fired Projects	141
		The Cross	141
		Stained Glass Glued Panel	142
		Working with Came	143
		Dalles	145
		Procedure	147
		A Sheet of Glass Is Blown	148

11. GLASS FROM
      OTHER LANDS   154

Diagrams   166

Glossary   171

Bibliography   177

Sources of Materials
      and Supplies   178

Index   181

KILN-FIRED GLASS

The beauty that haunts the edges of our being finds birth and life through the trained and sensitive hand. Without such hands, how much of truth and wonder would slip away as unborn, unshared shadows.

HUGH M. PEASE

1

Working With Glass

The well-known glass craftsman, Maurice Heaton, uses the term "glass slumping" to describe the process of firing glass in a kiln on a mold. Other descriptive names include glass sagging and glass bending.

Glass slumping involves firing flat pieces of glass in a mold to produce objects the shape of the mold although the glass does not reach a molten stage. The amount of heat required to accomplish this is an important factor and is covered in the chapter Firing Schedules.

In addition to the use of a mold that directs the contour of the glass, pieces may be fired flat directly on a kiln shelf.

The Glass Blank

"Glass blank" is the term used for glass that has been cut to the shape and size desired for the finished piece. It does not describe small pieces embossed on top of a blank.

Preparation

Before any design can be executed on glass using the basic techniques and their variations described in the following chapters, certain steps are to be followed when working with glass.

SELECTING THE GLASS

Strength in relation to the size of the glass is important. Glass is available in a number of thicknesses (strengths). Featherweight, sometimes used for framed pictures, can be used for such items as glass flowers but is not recommended for larger pieces. To be sure that the finished piece has sufficient strength for its size, there are limitations which must be observed.

The following are maximum sizes for objects that would have frequent handling and refer to both square and round blanks.

One Blank:

Single strength	6 inches
Double strength	8 inches
Plate and Crystal	15 inches

Two Blanks Laminated:

Two single strength	12 inches
One single and one double strength	15 inches
Two double strength	over 15 inches

Plate glass is available in ¼-, ⅜-, and ½-inch thicknesses. Crystal, which is not the same as lead crystal, comes in $7/32$- and $7/16$-inch thicknesses and is not as highly polished as plate glass. Glass thicker than ¼ inch would not be used except for some special reason and has not been used in the projects in this book.

Double-strength glass was used for many laminated pieces, especially for ashtrays, not out of necessity but to give added weight. A single blank of double-strength glass may be used for a large lampshade since it is rarely handled and it is desirable to lighten the load of the fixture.

All blanks to be combined for laminating should be from the same manufacturer. If this information is not available, laminate and fire two small blanks. Fractures will occur if they are not compatible. Unlike stained glass in which there is stress resulting from certain combinations, with a fracture showing up even months later, double- and single-strength glass will fracture by the time it has cooled if the coeficients of expansion are different.

TO CLEAN GLASS

After glass has been cut to size, clean with water and detergent. Handle the glass only at the edges after drying to prevent fingermarks on the surface of the blank. Hold the glass up to the light to check for any marks which might not have been removed.

BLANKS IN RELATION TO THE MOLD

Except where irregular shapes are planned, the blanks should be cut to fit the mold. The pieces may be smaller but not larger than the mold. Two or more blanks that are to be fired together should be exactly the same size if the end product is to give the appearance of a single piece of glass. If there is a slight variation in the pieces that have been intended to be the same size, the larger blank should be placed on top when laminating.

Irregularly shaped blanks can be cut and fired in any mold regardless of its shape. The blank will not lose its shape during the firing except for the contour change by slumping. It must not extend beyond the outer edge of the mold at any point. Color Plate 10, "Paisley," is a free-form bowl fired in an oval mold.

2

Equipment

Equipment needed for working with glass is available at ceramic supply stores and suppliers and mail-order houses that specialize in the needs of the glass craftsman. When purchased tools do not meet the requirements of the craftsman, they may be adjusted or made to meet a particular need. The following information will serve as a guide.

Kilns

The most efficient firing of glass is attained in a top-loading kiln or in a front-loading kiln that has an element in the door. However, the relationship of the motorist to his car is the same as of the glass craftsman to his kiln. All have their preferences.

CERAMIC

Some kilns have hot spots and cold spots. The chapter on firing schedules describes handling these problems. Many front-loading kilns do not have an element in the door. The area near the door is cooler than the rest of the interior of the kiln, which affects the edges of the fired piece nearest it. This can be offset by not using this part of the kiln, which, however, reduces the number of pieces that can be fired at one time. An even distribution of heat is achieved in most top-loading kilns. Figs. 1 and 2.

Fig. 1. The interior firing chamber of this kiln measured 13½ inches high by 14 inches in diameter before a 6½ inch collar was added. The portable pyrometer is inserted in a peephole plug. The kiln is located in a corner away from draft, ventilated as a firing begins.

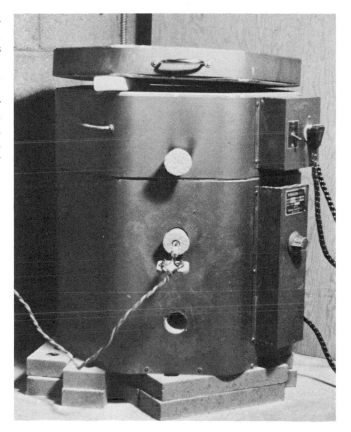

LARGE ENAMELING KILNS

Large enameling kilns with controls will fire glass as well as front-loading kilns, using the proper firing schedule.

SMALL ENAMELING KILNS

Small, inexpensive, one-speed enameling kilns that do not require special wiring, may be used to fire glass flat. Since the switch is limited to "on" and "off," the kiln heats up quickly. The "on" position is the same as high in other kilns. Firing glass on a mold in this kiln is not satisfactory most of the time. The fast heating causes distortion during the

6

Fig. 2. A heavy-duty kiln. The inside chamber measures 18x18x18 inches.

slumping and the fast cooling results in a very brittle, easily broken product. Fig. 3.

The Kiln Shelf

The kiln shelf used for pottery is heavy and retains heat longer than the glass when cooling. If no foot or pedestal is on the underside of the mold, that is, if the bottom of the mold is flat and rests on the kiln shelf, use supports of posts on their sides or small pieces of firebrick under the mold.

Fig. 3. A small enameling kiln without heat controls. No special wiring is needed. The inside chamber measures 7½ inches deep, 8½ inches wide, and 4 inches high. It may be used for small hangings made from stained glass and clear glass to which colorants have been applied.

Small shelves may be made of a fireproof, ceramic, acoustical material that comes in 2×4 foot and 4×4 foot sheets. It is very soft and porous, approximately ¾ inch thick, and can be cut with a sharp knife or saw. Having a large supply of small shelves is helpful when working with groups of people in a classroom. Fig. 145.

Cut a piece the desired shelf size from the described sheet. Rest on a kiln shelf that has been coated with dry high-fire kiln wash applied with a sifter. Fire with the white glazed side up. In a ceramic kiln, ventilate, with the switches on low for one hour. Turn the switches to high leaving the kiln ventilated an additional half hour, then close. Turn off when an 014 cone bends or the pyrometer reaches 1500 degrees F. The shelves will be stronger and less porous if they are fired to 2000 degrees F. but it is not necessary if they are to rest on a large kiln shelf. For one-speed kilns, rest the piece on firebrick or a shelf. Turn on for one hour, ventilated, then close and continue to fire for approximately three-quarters of an hour. Fire in a ventilated room.

Remove the shelf when cool and sand the white side to remove any loose particles. They will flake off easily. This is now the underside of the shelf. Paint the unglazed side, which the glass or mold will rest on, with a separating paste. Each time the shelf is used to fire glass flat, sift a thin film of high-fire kiln wash on it to attain a smooth finish on the underside. This application will assure complete separation and prevent pinpoints at the edges of the fired piece.

If a glass blank is fired flat on one of these shelves, bore a few small holes in it to allow air to escape that might otherwise be trapped and form a bubble. If the project to be fired is made up of small strips of glass such as in "Fish and Fowl," Color Plate 14, holes in the shelves are not needed, nor are they needed when used to support molds.

Align the support posts when stacking the shelves in the kiln to prevent excess strain on the shelf. Limit the size of the shelves to a maximum of 8 × 10 inches. These small shelves may rest on large kiln shelves which have had whiting or other separator sifted on them.

By having a number of shelves for articles to be fired flat, large projects made of many sections may be set up at one time and fired as kiln space becomes available. Also, stained glass or single- and double-strength glass to which colorants have been applied can be made for window hangings and Christmas tree ornaments in quantity and fired when convenient. The posts that separate the shelves may be purchased or made from firebrick.

FIREBRICK POSTS

Firebrick posts can be of any desired length. The other dimensions are one inch by one inch or more but not less. The posts should be cut so that they are flat at the top and bottom. Firebrick is soft and irregularities can be sanded. Dampen, but do not soak each post with a mixture of one part waterglass to two parts water. Allow to dry thoroughly. Fire to 1500 degrees F. on a kiln shelf that has been dusted with a separating powder before using, following the firing instructions for kiln shelves.

Pyrometer

A pyrometer is an instrument which measures the inside temperature of a kiln. A thermocouple is inserted inside the kiln and the temperature registers on a dial outside. If a pyrometer has not been installed at the factory, the thermocouple of one purchased may be inserted in a hole of the kiln's peephole plug. Fig. 1. A hole is easily bored into this soft material.

A screw below the face of the pyrometer is provided to adjust for calibration.

Pyrometric Cones

Pyrometric cones are made of a combination of materials in the shape of pyramids which deform at given temperatures. The rate of temperature rise has an effect upon the deformation of a cone. A particular cone will have a different deformation behavior under different firing schedules. The slower the temperature rise in the upper ranges of firing, particularly the last two hours, the lower the temperature will be when the cone deforms.

Because the rate of increase in temperature affects the performance of cones, it is important to note that cone numbers used in this book refer to small cones using the detailed firing schedule table in the chapter on Firing Schedules.

The pyrometers on the kilns used were calibrated to register 1425 degrees F. when a small 015 cone was bent but not otherwise deformed; that is to say, the triangular shape of the cone was still evident. If a fast firing is planned, a cone number which relates to a lower temperature would be needed.

Sifters

Sifters may be purchased or made from wire screening sold by the square foot. This material is sometimes referred to as sieve cloth in catalogs. Most are made of brass or bronze.

The sides of tuna fish or small pineapple cans serve as good frames for the screening. Cut a circle of screening one inch larger in diameter than the can. Press it against the outside of the can and solder together.

Use flux with the solder if the solder is not acid core. Acid core solder is best for brass. The size of the mesh is determined by the desired end result. Fine mesh, either 100 or 120, is needed for sifting dry separating powder on the mold or kiln shelf to give a smooth finish to the glass. If a coarser textured effect is wanted on the underside of the fired piece, make or buy a sifter using 30 or 50 mesh screening. The lower the number the coarser the screening. Fig. 4.

Small sifters, two inches in diameter and under, of 80 mesh screening are used for applying dry enamels and ices. The ingenious craftsman will make sifters of all sizes and shapes to aid the control and distribution of powders to achieve particular effects.

Tools

The tools for designs sgraffitoed into sifted powdered glass can be any of the wooden modeling tools used for clay. Wood carving and leather carving tools with the metal points sanded to a desired angle are helpful. Insert the sharp end of a needle into a cork and use the blunt end to scratch fine lines into a sprayed surface.

Wide-nosed pliers are needed to nip off excess small pieces of glass at the scored line. They are also used to sever scored narrow strips. Glass

Fig. 4. Two sizes of Japanese brushes, a straight glass cutter, wide-nosed pliers, and three sifters. The fine-mesh large sifter is used to apply separating powder. Its depth is an advantage over purchased sifters of this diameter.

Fig. 5. Decorating wheel, scrubber sponge, cork with needle for fine sgraffito work, grease pencil, tools for sgraffito designs.

cutters have three sizes of cutouts to assist in this operation if pliers are not available.

Circle cutters may be bought at glass equipment houses. Straight glass cutters may be bought at a hardware store.

A revolving decorating wheel with an eight-inch head allows the craftsman to turn a glass blank when applying a design without having to touch the glass. The wheel is used particularly when applying glaze with a slip trailer and when designing into dry powder.

Grease pencils and graphite pencils will write on glass. Figs. 4-6.

An electric engraver allows the craftsman to sign his work. Initials may also be scratched into opaque powdered glass before the glass is fired.

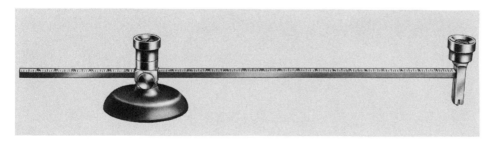

Fig. 6. The circle cutter.

Fig. 7. Equipment used when working with stained glass: soldering irons, solder, soldering paste, glass cutter, three thicknesses of came, wide-nosed pliers, hammer for cutting stained glass dalles, and two cutting knives.

The double-edged hammer, cames, and double-bladed knife in Fig. 7 are used when working with stained glass and are discussed in that chapter.

Electric Sprayers

Certain types of designing with powdered glass require the use of a sprayer with a compressor. It is used to dampen the powder to hold it intact. The glass may then be turned upside down so that the colorant is on the underside. This is done when laminating, to combine two blanks that have been decorated, the parts of which are to mesh. Also,

Fig. 8. A sprayer.

when a single blank is fired with the powdered glass on the underside, the spray acts to unify the particles. Hand pumped sprayers invariably emit an uneven coating with occasional droplets that disturb the powder. The alternatives to using a sprayer are discussed in the chapter Techniques in Laminating and Decorating Glass. The use of the sprayer is covered in the chapter Materials and How To Use Them.

Sprayers are available in many sizes. The small one shown in Fig. 8, with an adjustable nozzle, is adequate for spraying on glass since the area to be covered is small.

3

Materials and How To Use Them

Colorants

Some colorants discussed in this chapter were developed to be combined with materials other than glass, some for glass alone. Within this framework, there are materials compatible to or workable with some types of glass and not others. There is always an element of curiosity and anticipation when trying something new and then hoping for the best, but it is important to be aware of what not to combine.

GLASS COLORS—LIQUIDS

Glass glazes give transparent color to the glass. Many of these are pale. When used for laminations, apply a coating between the blanks and on top of the upper blank to strengthen the color.

Translucent glass glazes are handled the same as other glass glazes but are stronger in color, with the difference that while the finished piece emits light it is not transparent.

Glass enamels are used for designing and decorating. They are opaque.

POWDERED GLASS

Most of the colorants used in this book are powdered glass. The enamels are the same as those applied on metal. The ices are enamels adjusted in formula to be compatible to the surface of glass. Both transparent enamels and ices are pervious to light. Although these materials

14

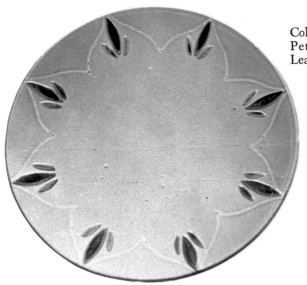

Color Plate 1. "Eight Petals and Sixteen Leaves."

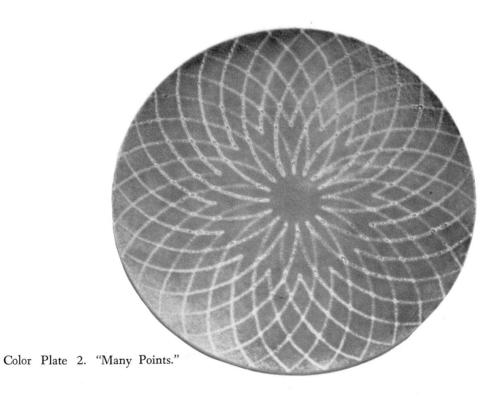

Color Plate 2. "Many Points."

Color Plate 3. "Bowl" by Michael and Frances Higgins.

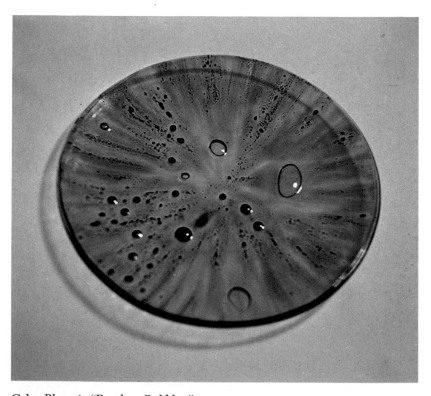

Color Plate 4. "Random Bubbles."

are available from a number of manufacturers, the color numbers and names used in this book refer to the opaque and transparent enamels and ices from the Thomas C. Thompson Company of Highland, Illinois. All may be used for lamination.

The following information relates to the handling of powdered glass fused to the surface of glass.

OPAQUE ENAMEL POWDERS

Many opaque powders may be fused to the glass surface if it is topped with a transparent clear ice (No. 815) or flux. The amount of opaque powder that is sifted on the glass and how much transparent ice is sifted on top are important. It is unlikely that a blank would be covered with an oqaque powder without removing some of it to create a design since it would remove the transparency that typifies glass. Whenever opaque powder is used, whether laminated or applied as a colorant for the surface of the blank, a light coating is recommended.

EMBOSSED PIECES—OPAQUE

Paint the pieces to be embossed with a film of squeegee oil, and sift the opaque powder over it. Unless the oil is applied first, the edges of a small piece of glass will have a lighter color than the rest of it. Sift enough powder to cover the surface but only that. If the application is too heavy, the powder will become a sheet of glass and may release from the piece to which it has been applied. This would happen only if a very excessive amount were used. Top this coating with the barest minimum of transparent clear ice. Hold an 80 mesh sifter in one hand and tap gently against the side of the sifter with one finger of the other hand. This is not a coating but only enough to see that the granules are present.

If a sprayer is available, spraying the pieces prevents the powders from being disturbed when placing them on the blank to which they are to be fused. No spray was used for the embossed pieces in this book. Handling and placing become routine.

EMBOSSED PIECES—ICES

A film of squeegee oil is applied to the glass piece and the ice is sifted over it. Use a heavier coating of this powder than when applying opaque powder. No additional topping is needed. Ices have been developed for glass.

When ices are combined with glass and fired to the temperature needed to achieve the desirable rounded edges on the finished piece, the high-fire series is needed. If low-fire ices are used and fired beyond 1100 degrees F. a loss in the depth of color is evident.

EMBOSSED PIECES—TRANSPARENT AND SOME OPAQUE ENAMELS

Transparent and some opaque enamels for metal are not compatible to the glass surface. They will chip off even when topped with transparent clear ice or low-fusing flux No. 426. This problem can be overcome. Coat the pieces to be embossed with squeegee oil, sift the enamel over the pieces and burn off the oil as in laminations. Invert the pieces so that the enamel touches the blank to which it is to be fused.

OTHER GLASS DECORATING POWDERS

A very fine powder is available that may be mixed with water for specific uses. This falls into the category of a liquid glaze. The glass blank or embossed piece may be painted with this glaze and fired if the high-fire series of these decorating colors is used. The opaque low-fire series of these powders mixed with water may be used to paint on a fired piece and refired to 1100 degrees F.

The high-fire series mixed with squeegee oil has been used for silk screen printing and is discussed in that chapter.

These very fine powders have a prefix of HF, LF, or HFT in front of their numbers. Most are opaque (HF and LF) and are so fine if sifted over oiled lines that the excess will not tap off. They may, however, be sifted dry on pieces to be embossed. They are compatible to glass without any topping of transparent ice or clear flux.

PAINTING MATERIALS—OPAQUE

Ceramic glazes, Versa colors, and glass enamels may be used to paint on glass.

Applying a Design With Oil

Work out the design on paper and place it under a glass blank. A Japanese brush or any brush that has a fine point is used to paint in the lines of the design with squeegee oil. Work where there is good light. Vegetable color may be added to give the oil color. This will burn out in the firing. Use the tip of the brush and dip frequently. If an excessive amount of oil gets on the blank, do not attempt to remove it as it will smear the glass. Corrections can be scratched off later.

When the design for one color has been applied with oil, sift the powdered glass over the oiled blank and tap off the excess. If more than one color is applied to one blank, use the same procedure for subsequent colors, the lightest color last. Figs. 50-53. Variations to this basic technique may be found in the chapter "Techniques for Laminating and Decorating Glass."

If the piece is to be laminated, the oil must first be baked off. Place the decorated blank in a cold oven and heat to 300 degrees F. Turn off and allow the glass to cool enough for easy handling. The combination of squeegee oil and powdered glass has now become a soft crust. Corrections can be made at this time by scratching off any excess.

If preferred, the oil may be burned off in the kiln. Place the blank on the mold in the kiln and turn kiln on high, ventilated. Leave on for about five minutes, then turn off.

If more than one color has been applied to a piece to be laminated, place a clear blank on the mold and top it with the decorated blank, colored side down. In the event that some of the powder of one color adhered to another color, it will not show up.

If the blank is not to be laminated, and an opaque powder has been used, sift transparent clear ice over the entire blank as described earlier

Fig. 9. The tulip is shiny. Red ice was applied to the flower and HFT-green was sifted on the stem. The background is frosted plate glass. The cornflower is colored with a turquoise ice and the stem is colored with HFT-green. Transparent clear powder was sifted over the entire decorated piece to give it a shiny surface.

in this chapter. Plate glass will crystalize and have a frosted appearance without this application. In some cases, this is desirable. Fig. 9.

Slip Trailing With Glazes

As shown in Fig. 10, Earl McCutchen, of the University of Georgia, uses this technique among others to design on glass. The potter is very much at home with a slip trailer. He uses a glaze frit that melts at a lower temperature than sheet glass and to which ceramic glaze coloring agents are added.

Frits are used liquid and dry. Liquid frit is sprayed or trailed. Dry application is made by tapping from folded paper to control the application.

Fig. 10. Earl McCutchen trailing a glaze on the blank.

Fig. 11. This fifteen-inch tray is laminated using black, white and brown glaze, the white applied with a slip trailer. By Earl McCutchen.

Color Samples

Make sample strips of colorants as they are acquired. Use strips of single- or double-strength glass about three inches wide and eight inches long. Paint a ¾-inch wide band with squeegee oil, leaving a margin to write in the color number. Sift a colorant on top and tap off the excess. Cover it with cardboard and proceed with the remaining colors to be sampled. Color samples for liquid colorants can be made on separate strips. Write in the color numbers with a black liquid enamel or any opaque glaze. On the left, over part of the color samples, place a strip of the same type of glass about one inch wide and the length of the strip. If the powders are not ices or other powders compatible to glass, sift a thin application of transparent clear ice or a glass flux over the entire strip. Place on a kiln shelf which has been prepared with a separating powder or paste and fire along with a kiln load. Fig. 12.

Sample strips will indicate the limitations of the various types of materials. The lack of compatibility of the transparent enamels to glass, unless laminated, is revealed on the underside of the strip. While the uncovered surface is intact, held by the transparent clear application, fractures show on the underside and will chip off in time. Some few opaque blues and greens will show evidence of this. In those cases, use a thinner coating of the colored powder. All yellows, browns, oranges, and reds tested were compatible to the surface with the barest minimum topping of transparent clear ice or clear flux.

Sample strips of ices and the HF, LF, and HFT series are helpful although they are known to be compatible with glass and no type of flux

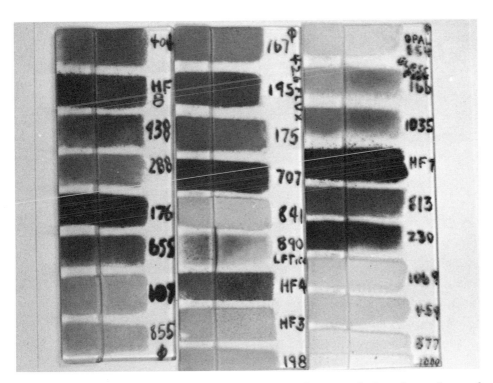

Fig. 12. A few strips of color samples, showing the colorant applied to the surface and the lamination to the left on the strip.

is needed on top. The strips will show the effect lamination has on the color. There is also a change in this series between using it as a liquid or sifted dry.

Observing the sample strips, none of the 46 transparent enamels tested can be used on the surface of glass except Lawn Green. At present, the color number is 160. It can be used as an ice except that a very light sifting of transparent clear ice is applied on top.

There are other powdered glass fluxes that may be substituted for transparent clear ice. Some release from plate glass, but otherwise they are satisfactory.

Glass glazes that are transparent, translucent glass glazes, and opaque glass enamels, all liquids, have colors unrelated to the end product when fired. Sample strips of these glazes will aid the craftsman, since some glazes will bubble when laminated. In addition to using the sample strip for these materials to indicate color, it will also reveal their behavior.

Opaque glass enamels are used to paint designs for laminations and on the surface of glass. The difference in the results of their use and of the combination of squeegee oil with enamels for metal is that glass enamels give a painted look. It is entirely a matter of preference for the craftsman to decide.

Other Materials

Screening, foil, glass chips, wire, and many other materials may be laminated between two or more layers of glass. Catalogs list a number of materials developed to be used with glass for special effects.

There is always the problem of compatibility when combining unrelated materials. Fiberglass threads dipped in opaque liquid enamels, glass threads, and chips of glass from some bottles present no problem. Foreign materials such as wire, screening, aluminum foil, and many other nonglass scraps that the craftsman will undoubtedly experiment with will prove successful if handled properly. Others will result in fractures. The foreign materials must be smooth and flat. Foil may be crushed and then

Fig. 13. Fifteen-inch square laminated tray using foil, wire, glaze, paper, and stain. The glass is patterned with thin lines. By Earl McCutchen.

flattened. Thin wire may be bent into shapes, but it is best not to overlap it. Unless it is planned to have the material burn out during the firing, such as mica which will leave a bubble, it should be known if the material will withstand the heat required to fire glass.

Use of a Sprayer

A thin liquid sprayed over a blank that has been coated with powdered glass, solidifies the coating and, if it is to be laminated, removes the air in the dry application that would otherwise be trapped. A sprayer is a convenience although similar results can be achieved with alternative procedures. (See chapter Techniques for Laminating and Decorating Glass.)

A fine spray of any of the mixtures suggested requires the use of a sprayer with a compressor or one with a built-in motor and adjustable nozzle. Hand-pumped sprayers will inevitably emit an uneven coating with occasional droplets that will disturb the dry powder.

Agar, gum arabic, Klyr-fire, and flat beer are some of the sprays used on powdered enamels.

Agar is used full strength. If beer is used, shake well before using to remove the possibility of foaming. Mix one part Klyr-fire to two parts water. If this mixture does not hold the powder use less water. Other spraying materials are available.

A light sifting of opaque enamel is applied to a glass blank, the design sgraffitoed and then sprayed. The enamel is first dampened with the spray from a distance of about four feet. Once damp, the spraying continues at closer range to wet the powder. A side to side motion is used rather than a circular path. When dry, the glass may be fired with the powder on the underside. Color Plate 10.

Whenever the powder is to be fired next to the mold, a coating of high-fire kiln wash must be sifted on the mold, which was first coated with a paste of whiting and water or Mold-coat and water.

To achieve an even light dusting of an opaque powder, spray the clean blank first. Then sift the powdered glass over the wet blank and allow it to dry thoroughly. Tap off the excess, holding the blank on end. Brush off any loose powder with a Japanese brush. The coating will be thin and even unless the spraying has been exaggerated over part of the blank. Sgraffito designs may be worked into this coating. Tap or blow off the excess powder while working.

For a two-part design in which each of two blanks is to be prepared for lamination, spraying allows the upper half of the design to be turned upside down. Figure 74. An alternative to the use of the sprayer in this case is to prefire each part flat on a kiln shelf to 1150 degrees F. Refire the combined blanks on a mold.

If a sprayer is not used, a single blank that is to be fired with the powder on the underside may be prefired flat on a kiln shelf and then fired on a mold.

Clear Flux on Top of Glass

Clear flux applied on top of a piece to be fired gives a shiny finish and prevents the possibility of finger marks and smudges showing up that were not evident before firing. Soft-, medium-, and hard-fusing clear fluxes are available.

Soft-fusing flux may be used on rolled stained glass if the surface is dull, which is probably due to a separator embedded in the glass. This occurs sometimes in pebbly sheet glass. Soft-fusing flux No. 426 may be used on plate, single or double strength glass. Transparent clear ice is a flux compatible to the surface of glass and is best for sifting over opaque enamel powders to prevent them from chipping off.

The use of clear flux is for the craftsman to determine. If the glass has been thoroughly cleaned and carefully handled, and if the kiln has been properly ventilated, the flux would be used only to achieve a high gloss on the surface of the finished piece. However, it does give assurance that there will not be any unwanted marks on the fired glass.

Bases for Mixing Enamels

The *Ceramic Industries Magazine* has supplied the following definition for flux. "Flux lowers the fusion point of any mixture in which it is present. In connection with glass decorating, a flux is a prepared low-melting glass, usually colorless, which may be mixed with pigments or oxides to produce vitrifiable coatings on glass. A typical flux for glass is: 50% lead oxide, 35.2% silica, 10.8% borax oxide, and 3.2% sodium bicarbonate."

Certain combinations of materials are used for specific reasons. Lead and potash in controlled quantities are added for brilliance. Borax and soda or potash are used in determining the coefficient of expansion of the mixture. The depth of color is controlled by the amount of pigment or oxide that is added to the frit or flux. The addition of tin oxide changes a transparent enamel to opaque.

A frit is a chemical composition that acts as a flux and is adjusted for particular needs. It is available in a wide range of coefficients of expansion.

Frit No. 3396 is available from a number of distributors and is a good base for enamels for glass. The proportions vary with the density of color desired. From two to five percent of a batch is the oxide, the frit being the basic ingredient. It may be used dry or mixed with water and sprayed or used with a slip trailer. If the mixture is sprayed it should be thinner than when it is applied with a slip trailer.

Transparent clear ice No. 815 when mixed with powders that are developed to be fired to a higher temperature than that needed for glass, gives a more transparent end product than when mixed with frit number 3396.

The workable mixtures are almost endless. They will not be the same color when fired to 1425 degrees F. as they would be when fired to their proper cones.

A Few Examples

One part George Fetzer opaque stain when mixed with three parts frit No. 3396 will result in an excellent color and is compatible to the surface of glass. It may be mixed with water or sifted in dry form. All of the stains were not tested. Pink stain number 562 fires to a good soft rose color and gives best results when sprayed or applied with a slip trailer.

Equal parts of transparent low-fire crackle glaze, which is for cone 010 and was developed by Amaco, and Thompson's transparent clear ice No. 815 result in a translucent color and are compatible to the glass surface. Color number 942, foliage green, fires to a good turquoise on the glass surface and becomes a little bubbly when laminated. The few opaque crackle glazes tested had a lack of color when mixed with No. 815 but stronger with equal parts glaze and frit 3396.

4

Molds

To give a glass object contour, the flat blank is placed on a mold and fired in a kiln. The firing schedule is determined by the type of glass used. When the firing is completed, the glass has taken on the shape of the mold. It has not become molten but only soft enough to slump into the shape dictated by the mold. The sharp edges of the glass have become smooth in the process.

Molds have a major effect on the finished piece. A mold that has detail, such as one with a fluted pattern, will supply the design, and only the addition of a colorant to the glass is needed. Fig. 14. Stained glass requires only the cutting of the glass to the shape of the mold. Fig. 15.

Molds manufactured especially for glass are available. However, they can be made inexpensively using various materials. In addition, poured greenware, although not made for this purpose, may be used if it complies with the conditions required for any mold used for slumping glass. The two major requirements for molds that have contour, regardless of the material used, are that the inside bottom of the mold be flat if the fired piece is to sit well on a table and that the walls have a gentle slope.

Greenware

Greenware made from slip, which is a clay mixed with a suspending agent and combined with water, is poured into a plaster mold. After fifteen or twenty minutes the excess slip is poured off. After another thirty to forty-five minutes the formed clay slip is removed and allowed to dry. The larger the finished piece, the thicker the walls must be, which is the reason for the variation in the time before removing the formed clay.

Fig. 14. Fluted plate, bisque-fired greenware mold. The blank is cut to fit the inner point of the scalloped edge.

When poured greenware is purchased, if possible select a piece that needs no patching up. However, to correct any slight concave curve to make the bottom flat, use a damp sponge and rub gently around the outer edge of the center until the bottom is level. Allow to dry before bisque firing. If the center of the bottom is convex, that is, slightly higher than the rest of the bottom, no correction is necessary.

Fire greenware in a kiln to an 013 cone or about 1550 degrees F., using the firing schedule provided in the booklet that comes with the kiln. Some ceramic supply shops that sell greenware will bisque-fire it for a nominal fee, but unless a separate firing is done, the piece will probably be fired to approximately 1850 degrees F. or an 06 pyrometric cone. The recommended 1550 degrees is above the temperature required for glass. By not firing the piece to its usual 06 cone, the clay is more porous, which is desirable for glass molds.

Fig. 15. Bisque-fired greenware mold. The stained glass owl is a soft green. The outline below the head was scored with a gentle curve to prevent decapitation when severing. The tail was eliminated as this would be the same as overlapping the edge of the mold. If it had been included, the pull of the glass as it cooled would have caused a fracture.

Bore several small holes into the bottom of the bisque-fired piece. If the holes are larger than $\frac{1}{16}$ of an inch, patch them with a paste made of water and a separating powder. Use a pin to open them up if they are completely plugged with the paste. Do not put holes in dry greenware, as it may crack.

The size and shape of the mold determine the best placement for the holes. If the inside of the mold has vertical grooves or curves, holes may not be necessary. Put holes in all molds whose inner walls are smooth. A small bowl that has a base of $3\frac{1}{2}$ inches in diameter, would require two holes placed near the rim of the bottom of the mold.

Wax Impressions for Clay Molds

Many manufactured objects have a foot or pedestal on the bottom of the outside. Because of this, the inside of the piece makes a more desirable model from which to make an impression.

To obtain an impression from the inside of an object to be duplicated, first fill it with water to see that the table or counter on which it is resting is level. Pour off the water and fill the piece with melted wax. Wax is an ideal material because it can be scraped to level the bottom, carved to embed a design on the sides or bottom, and the clay releases easily from it.

Do not hurry the cooling of the poured wax as this may cause uneven shrinkage. As the wax cools, the center will become slightly concave. This does not matter as long as the outer part remains level. However, the cavity may be filled in with additional melted wax after the model hardens.

To remove the wax from its mold, run hot water over the outside long enough to allow the wax to detach itself from the inside. Set the wax model on the table to test the flatness of the bottom. A straight-edged knife will remove any unwanted contour.

If grooves or other designs are planned, they may be carved into the wax with a knife or tool. A V-shaped leather carving tool lends itself to vertical grooves. This may be done on the clay itself when it is at the leather-hard stage. If the mold is to have a raised design in the bottom, it is best to carve it into the wax. The wax model is the positive. Fig. 16.

Prepare a board for wedging the clay. A piece of coarsely woven cloth, such as unbleached muslin, thumbtacked to a piece of plywood, will serve the purpose. Clay is wedged with the same motion used to knead dough. This is done to remove air pockets from the clay. If they are not removed, they will explode during the firing.

Place two strips of wood, approximately one-quarter inch thick, parallel and the distance apart required for the size mold planned. For molds larger than nine inches in diameter, roll the clay thicker. Roll out the clay, lift, and drape it over the wax model. Press the clay firmly against the model. Trim off the excess but allow for a rim. After the clay has set for several hours or more, depending on how moist the clay is, carefully remove it from the wax. If it has become distorted to the extent that it will not hold its shape, return it to the wax model. It is not dry enough to remove. If the clay is allowed to remain on the model until it starts to shrink, the clay will crack. Correct any slight distortions to the

Fig. 16. Wax model. The wax was poured into a bowl. When cold the model was released when hot water was run over the outside of the bowl. The design was carved into the bottom of the wax and a slab of clay draped over it. See text.

shape resulting from handling when the clay is separated from the model. When leather-hard smooth the inside wall of the clay with a damp sponge if necessary. Then use a thin nail to make several air escape holes in the bottom of the mold. Carve grooves from the holes to the edge of the outside bottom of the mold.

After the clay has thoroughly dried, which can take several days, fire to an 012 cone or 1550 degrees F. The fired piece, Fig. 17.

Clay Pinchpots

Pinchpots can make interesting molds. Wedged clay (see above) is shaped into a ball and then formed by hand without additional equipment.

Fig. 17. The fired piece and the mold.

Press a hole into the center of a ball of clay and start pressing the sides to form a planned shape. As the walls are pressed thin, if desired the clay may be placed over an object of similar size to shape the contour. Do not leave the clay on the object. Shape and smooth the inner wall. It is necessary that both the inside and outside of the bottom be flat. When leather hard put in the air escape holes and carve the inside wall as desired.

Trim the outside bottom of the leather-hard mold, leaving a rim that becomes a small foot for the mold, or groove a shallow channel from the air escape hole to the outer edge of the bottom of the mold.

The slight irregularities that are present when clay is shaped by hand add to the individuality of glass pieces fired in molds made by this process. Fig. 18.

Fig. 18. The pinchpot and the fired piece. Transparent powdered glass gave color to this laminated piece. Liquid transparent glaze may be used between the blanks and on top of the upper blank.

Carved Firebrick

A small Chianti bottle with a rounded bottom was laid on its side and the outline drawn on a firebrick. An iced-tea spoon was used to carve into the brick. As the carving proceeded, the cavity was checked by resting the bottle on the brick until the hole was a little deeper than the radius of the bottle at its widest point. The curve of the neck was completed after a hole was carved into the part where the end of the bottle would bend. The depth of this hole should be the same as the deepest part of the main part of the bowl. Fig. 19.

Fine patching cement, used to patch the walls of a kiln, may be applied to the mold to smooth or correct any part of the carving as needed.

When carving is completed, dampen the mold with water before applying a separating paste of either whiting or Mold-coat mixed with water. To obtain a smooth finish on the outside of the fired piece, sift a

Fig. 19. The bottle, the iced-tea spoon used for carving, and the carved firebrick.

Fig. 20. The bottle and its relationship to the carved mold.

Fig. 21. The spoonholder or ashtray before and after firing. Some Chianti bottles are made with a flat base. The rounded base fires better.

thin film of high-fire kiln wash on the mold before each firing. Figs. 20 and 21.

Molds for firing larger bottles may be purchased from glass supply distributors and mail-order houses.

To make larger molds from firebrick, use a cement that withstands high heat to hold two firebricks together and carve out the shape. Sauereisen #31 (see Sources of Materials and Supplies) is a very good cement for this use. Patching cement intended for patching kiln walls does not work.

Use of the Outside of a Mold

Glass may be placed on top of the outside of a mold and fired. If the mold is being used for the first time, it is prepared as usual by applying the separator paste. Dampen the mold, apply a paste of whiting or Mold-coat mixed with water, smooth if necessary with a damp sponge, and sift a layer of high-fire kiln wash over it. Allow to dry before using. In subsequent firings only an application of the dry powder is needed.

Measure the outside of the mold from side to side including the curve of the mold at the center. The actual dimension of the mold shown in Fig. 22 is 7¼ inches. The measurement that determines the diameter of the glass that will cover the outside of the bowl mold is 8 inches.

Fig. 22. The blank, coated with HFT-yellow powder, resting on the underside of a bisque-fired greenware plate.

Fig. 23. The mold and the fired piece. The design, which is on the underside of the mold, is transferred to the plate-glass blank.

In Fig. 23, the mold is the design. HFT-yellow was sifted on a blank of plate glass and centered on top of the outside of the mold. The size of the blank was obtained by measuring the size of the mold including the depth through its center.

Preparing the Mold

Before firing a glass object, the surface with which the glass will come in contact requires the application of a separator or parting agent that prevents the glass from sticking to the surface.

The choice of the separator and the best method of its application are determined by the surface to which it is applied.

For glass to be fired flat on a kiln shelf, sift an even layer of high-fire kiln wash on the shelf. Use a fine mesh sifter for a smooth surface or a coarse sifter for a pebbly surface.

Prepare shallow molds that have only a slight contour, such as for plates, in the same way as for firing flat.

All molds with any depth require the application of a separator paste. Although it is not an absolute necessity, in addition to the paste, sift a light coating of high-fire kiln wash on the mold before each firing. It is not necessary to reapply the paste except to touch up a damaged area.

Make a thin paste by mixing whiting or Mold-coat with water. Dampen the mold. Paint or spray the paste on the mold. Before the paste is dry, smooth it with a damp sponge if needed. Then sift on a coating of high-fire kiln wash.

Designing With a Separator

A smooth mold may be given an interesting detail by painting a design on the mold with a separator paste. Draw the planned design on the inside wall or bottom of a mold with a pencil. Make a thin paste with water and whiting. Paint in the design with the paste, building it up to the thickness desired. The thicker the relief design in the mold the deeper the depression will be in the glass fired on it. The edges of the design should have a gentle slope. Additional detail may be scratched into the body of the design while the paste is still damp. Before the glass is placed on top of the mold allow it to dry. Sift a light coating of high-fire kiln wash over the mold before using.

Colorants may be added to the glass blank with no additional decorating. Initials in the bottom of a mold give a personal touch to a purchased mold. They may be removed after firing by wetting the mold and wiping until the design releases.

The kiln shelf can serve as a flat mold. Sift a heavy layer of separating powder on the shelf. Carve into the soft powder with a tool or depress the powder with small carved objects such as carrots, soap, etc. Shaped wire is an effective material for designing into the dry powder. Place the glass blank on the designed shelf and fire to 1375 degrees F. Liquid colorants may be painted on top of the glass or opaque powder sifted on top or applied to the underside as explained in the section, Use of a Sprayer, in chapter three.

5

Cutting Glass

To get the greatest mileage from a glass cutter, the wheel of the cutter should be kept well lubricated. Kerosene, with a thin oil added, is recommended. The proportion of kerosene to oil is about 10 parts kerosene to one part oil. Light machine oil or thin salad oil will do. Straight cutters should be stored in a jar in enough lubricant to cover the wheel.

To oil a circle cutter, paint the glass with the lubricant in a circle in the path of the cutter.

When cutting single- or double-strength glass a minimum allowance at the edge of the glass is about one-quarter inch. For heavier glass, such as the thick part of hand-blown stained glass and plate glass, a minimum of ¾ inch from the edge should be allowed. The larger the margin when cutting heavy glass, the easier it will be to sever the piece from the glass from which it is being cut.

Do not score glass over a hard surface. About eight thicknesses of newspaper will give the necessary bounce. If a great deal of work is planned, a padded cutting board is recommended. To prepare the board, use a piece of ¾ inch plywood, two by four feet, and pad it with three layers of flannel, topped with unbleached muslin. Smooth the layers and attach them to the plywood at its edges using a stapling gun or small tacks.

Using a Straight Glass Cutter

To cut a piece of glass, first mark the place to be scored with a grease pencil. Position the wheel of the straight glass cutter on this line and put

38

a ruler against the cutter. Score along the penciled line. (The word score is used because the glass is not actually cut.) Do not go over the scored line. Fig. 24.

The sound the cutter makes when the proper pressure is applied will become familiar with practice. If there is no sound, the scoring has not taken place. The surface has not been scratched. If too much pressure is applied, slightly chipped edges will result. Also, this is not good for the cutter. After a few attempts, the smallest amount of pressure needed to make the sound of scoring will be learned.

If the scored straight line is not close to the edge of the glass the severance is achieved without turning the glass. For single- and double-strength glass, place a finger or the ball end of the glass cutter under the center of the scored line at the edge of the glass. Cup the free hand over the scored line and using quick equal pressure at both sides of the score, snap the glass apart. Figs. 25 and 26. The scored line may also be snapped at the edge of a table. Fig. 27. For heavy glass, the same procedure is followed except that, if the piece is large, put a sheet over a rug and work on the floor. Score the line, place the ball end of the cutter at the edge of the glass in the center of the line, and using one hand on each side of

Fig. 24. For single- or double-strength glass, measure and draw the line to be cut with a grease pencil. Place the cutting wheel of a straight glass cutter on drawn line and bring ruler up to it. Score along the line. Work on a padded surface or on newspaper as described in the text.

Fig. 25. Place finger under the center of the scored line.

Fig. 26. Cup the other hand over the scored line and press, using equal pressure on both sides of the line. This step may be accomplished by turning the glass over and pressing along the scored line.

Fig. 27. If the sheet of glass is not too large to handle, the scored line may be snapped at the edge of a table.

the scored line, snap apart with quick equal pressure on both sides. Figs. 28 to 30.

For small pieces such as petals where uniformity of size is needed, draw parallel lines on the glass with a grease pencil the desired distance

Fig. 28. To cut a large heavy sheet of plate glass, work on the floor. Cover carpeting or layers of newspaper with a sheet, and score as for single- and double-strength glass.

Fig. 29. Place the ball end of the glass cutter under the scored line (the scored side up). Press with both hands using equal pressure on both sides of the line.

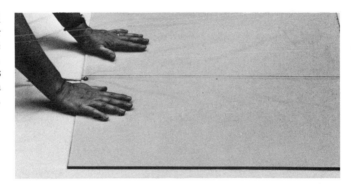

Fig. 30. The severed piece.

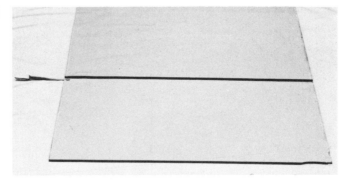

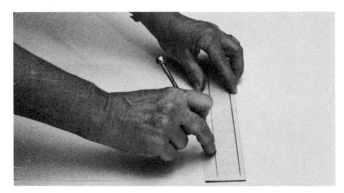

Fig. 31. If a number of small pieces of glass of the same size are needed, draw guide lines on a piece of glass where the scored lines are to intersect.

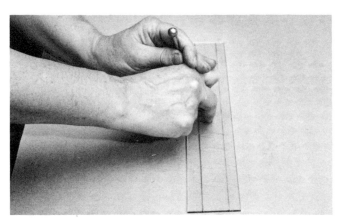

Fig. 32. To give better control if needed use pressure with one hand and guide with the other.

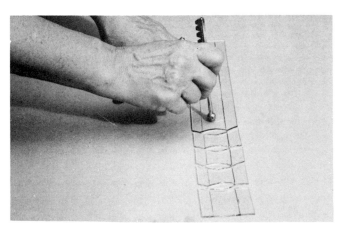

Fig. 33. Turn the glass over and tap over the scored lines.

apart. The lines are a guide for the intersection of the scores. Figs. 31 and 32. Score the glass as planned, turn over, and tap over the scored lines with the ball end of the glass cutter. Fig. 33.

To cut large irregular shapes from glass, especially plate glass, Fig. 34, draw the desired shape on paper. Place this pattern under the piece to be cut and follow these lines with the glass cutter. Or lines may be traced on the glass over the pattern or around a mold with a grease pencil and then scored on the lines. Avoid lifting the cutter more than necessary

Fig. 34. To cut an irregular shape from plate glass or other glass, mark the outline on the glass with a pencil.

and then only in an area where the contour of the line is the least curved. In case the actual mold is used, score inside the penciled line to allow for the thickness of the mold.

Turn the glass and tap firmly over the scored lines. Turn again so that the scored side is up. Score four lines from near, but not touching, the original scoring, to the outer edges of the excess glass. Turn once again and tap over the lines to sever the planned piece. Bite off any small pinpoints of glass that remain with wide-nosed pliers. Pinpoints are the result of incomplete tapping along the outline or where the cutter was lifted during the scoring, thus making possible a change in the angle of the cutter. Figs. 35 through 39.

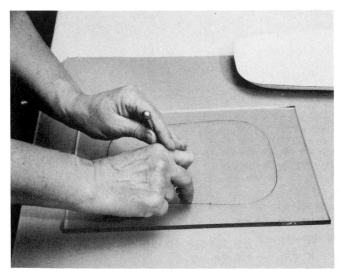

Fig. 35. Score along the marked line using both hands if necessary to guide the cutter. If the cutter is lifted as the scoring proceeds, choose a straight part of the line, if there is any. If the actual mold was used for the pattern, score just inside the penciled line to allow for the thickness of the rim of the mold.

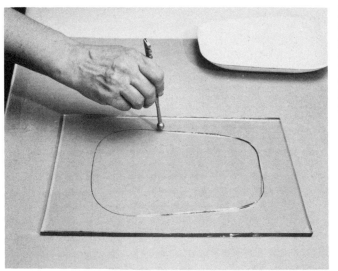

Fig. 36. Turn the glass over and, if using plate glass, tap over the scored line with the ball end of the cutter. Single- and double-strength glass may be pressed with the finger.

Fig. 37. Turn the glass back to the surface on which it was originally scored and score the glass at three or four places around the shape. Do not go all the way to the scored line. Leave about one quarter of an inch between the scored piece and these lines.

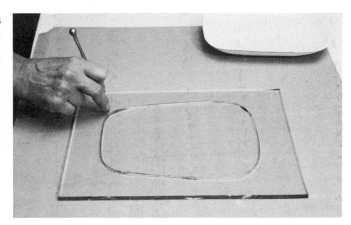

Fig. 38. Turn once again to the side on which the shape was tapped or pressed and tap the lines.

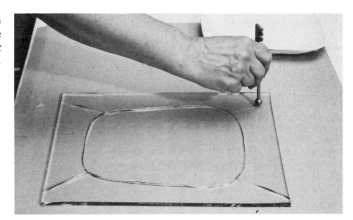

Fig. 39. The irregular shape severed.

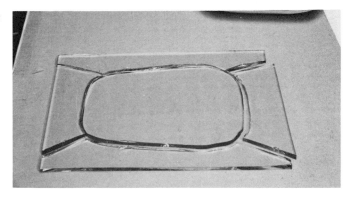

Cutting Circles

Position the circle cutter on the glass with an allowance for waste at the edges. Paint lubricant around the approximate path of the cutter. Score the glass. Turn the glass over and press or tap over the scored line making sure that some separation takes place, although this will not go all the way through. Pressing with the finger is preferred because it results in a smooth edge when severed. However, this cannot be done when using heavy glass or when the score is very close to the edge. Figs. 40 and 41.

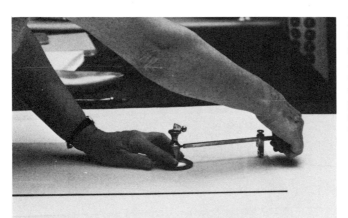

Fig. 40. A circle cutter is a necessary tool to make a perfect circle. Allow about a half inch edge to assure easy severence. The thicker the glass the farther the edge should be from the piece to be severed.

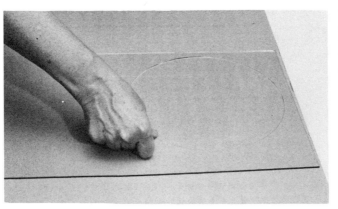

Fig. 41. For single- and double-strength glass, turn the glass over and press along the scored circle. If plate glass is used it will be necessary to tap over the score.

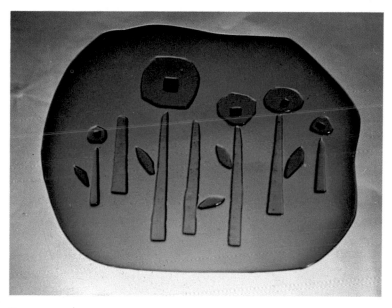

Color Plate 5. "Free Form."

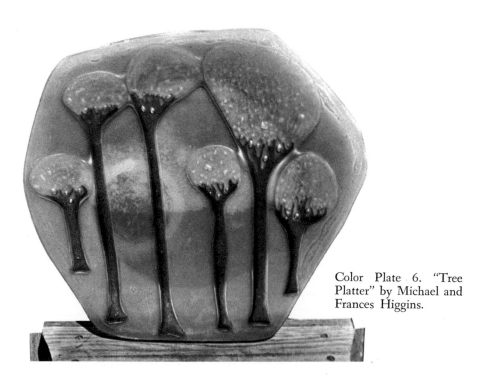

Color Plate 6. "Tree Platter" by Michael and Frances Higgins.

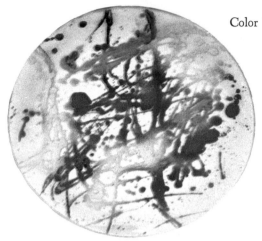

Color Plate 7. "A Happening."

Color Plate 8. "Candlelight," a 15-inch silk screen-printed bowl.

Color Plate 9. "Three Trees," another example
of the technique used in Color Plate 1.

Color Plate 10. "Paisley."

Color Plate 11. "Plate" by Michael and Frances Higgins.

Fig. 42. Turn the glass over again so that the scored side is up. Score four lines from near the scored circle to the edge of the sheet of glass.

Turn glass so that the scored side is up and, with a straight cutter, score three or four lines from near the rim of the circle to the edge of the sheet of glass. Turn once again and press or tap this set of lines. The circle will separate when the straight lines are tapped. If any small pieces remain along the edge of the circle they may be bitten off with wide-nosed pliers. Figs. 42 through 44.

Fig. 43. Turn over again and tap or press the scored lines.

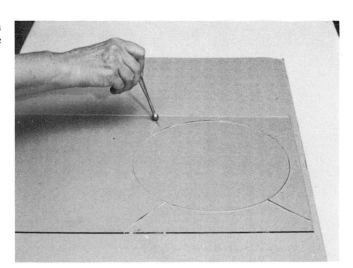

48

Fig. 44. The severed piece.

To Correct Rough Edges

The cut edges of glass will become smooth when fired. To smooth noticeable irregularities, rub them with a piece of abrasive material under water. Wet belts on elaborate equipment are the most effective way to smooth edges. In lieu of this type of machinery, a motor-driven belt sander may be used and water dribbled over the wet belt at intervals. The need for this is greater for plate glass than for thinner glass. If no equipment is available, purchase a wet belt, cut it into strips and attach a strip to a piece of wood. Sand the edges while holding the glass under water or allow water to dribble over it from a spigot. Another abrasive material used for this purpose is a fine carborundum stone.

When using wide-nosed pliers to remove any small pieces of glass from the blank, place pliers at the scored line and snap off the excess, using a downward motion with the scored line on the upper side of the blank.

Position of the Cutter

A very necessary rule to follow when scoring glass is to keep the cutting wheel straight. The wheel must not slant to one side. If it was a knife cutting a slice of cake, the cut would be straight down. The other angle of the cutter does not matter. Specifically, the cutter may slant toward you or away from you or straight up. However, the position should be constant once the scoring is started. Practice on a scrap of glass until scoring is achieved using the minimum pressure to scratch the surface.

How the cutter is held in the hand is up to the craftsman. A diagram is provided on the box-cover of most cutters showing the correct position. Follow the instructions. If a large amount of cutting is done a comfortable position will be acquired. Most diagrams show the cutter being held between the second and third finger with pressure from these fingers on top of the holder, with the thumb providing pressure from underneath. Fig. 45.

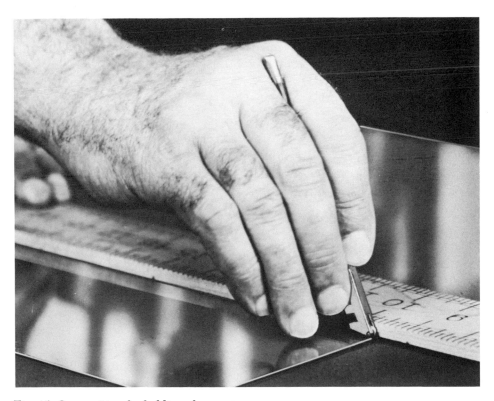

Fig. 45. One position for holding glass cutter.

Fig. 46. Chips of glass from a blue bottle were fired between two blanks for this 14-inch diameter bowl.

Breaking Up a Bottle

To break a bottle into small pieces for sandwiching between two blanks, wrap the bottle in aluminum foil, leaving the ends open and the sealed edges placed lengthwise. Put in a cold oven and heat to 500 degrees F. Keep the oven on and allow the bottle to remain in the oven for at least 20 minutes. Fill the sink with cold water. The bottle will remain intact when it is plunged into the cold water but will have multiple fractures. Light tapping will separate the particles. Most green bottles are made of glass that is compatible to single- and double-strength glass. Do not use the "no deposit throw-away" soda bottles.

Figure 46 shows the use of chips from a bottle.

6

Techniques For Laminating and Decorating Glass

Lamination

When two or more blanks of glass are combined and fired in a kiln, they fuse in the firing. This is called laminated glass. Small pieces of glass placed on top of one or more thicknesses of glass create an embossed design. Small pieces of glass may be placed on top of the blank, between two blanks, or on the underside of the glass blank. Fusing of the pieces, including the embossed designs, takes place in a single firing, although in isolated cases two firings are involved.

If the only reason for laminating two blanks the same size were to give strength to the end product, one blank the proper thickness would suffice. However, many interesting results are possible through the variety of techniques used in designing laminated pieces and this is a major consideration in using this process.

Compatibility of Glasses

Many formulas are used in the manufacture of glass. In laminating, the pieces must be compatible or fractures will result. Compatibility of glasses means having the same coefficient of expansion.

To illustrate, the designed glass is placed on a mold in a cold kiln, fired according to a schedule and not removed until the kiln has cooled. Viscosity increases as cooling takes place. If the combined blanks depart from their softened stage at the same time the glasses are said to be compatible, i.e., the coefficients of expansion (and contraction) are the same.

51

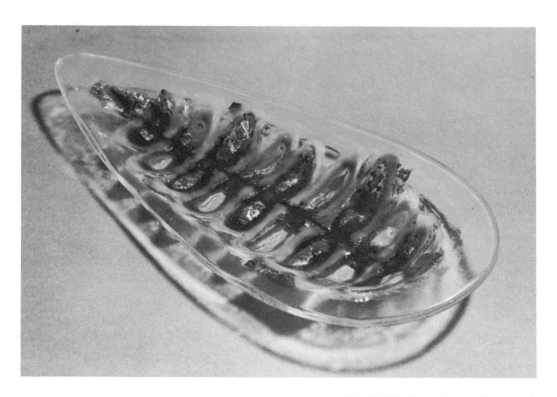

Fig. 47. Twelve-inch tray, laminated, using blues and grays with metallic luster. By Earl McCutchen.

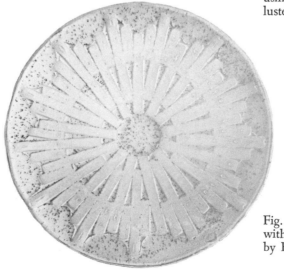

Fig. 47A. Ten-inch diameter plate with glass strips to form the design, by Earl McCutchen.

Since the pieces have fused in the firing, if one piece hardens before the other as cooling takes place, a fracture occurs. If the strain or pull is slight, the fracture may not take place for several days or even longer. To avoid the possibility of combining glasses that are not compatible, buy sheets of glass large enough so that all of the parts that will be used for the lamination can come from it. Compatibility of stained glass is discussed in that chapter.

Most single-strength glass is compatible to plate glass.

Applying the Design With Oil

The chapter Materials and How To Use Them gives in detail information that will prove helpful before using the following instructions.

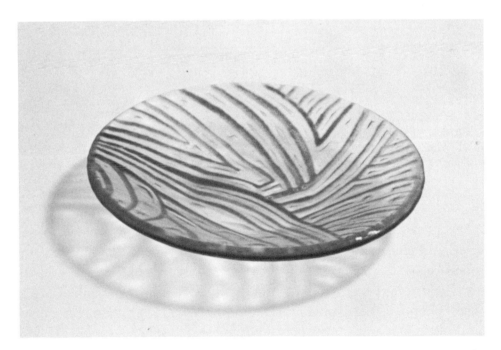

Fig. 48. "Gentle Breeze." The lines are painted in with oil, opaque olive green powder is sifted over it, and the excess is tapped off. The oil is burned off in a 300 degree F. oven before the blank is placed on a mold and topped with a matching blank.

Fig. 49. "Brace and Bit." The same procedure is followed as for Fig. 48 when applying the design. A light application of transparent clear ice or flux is sifted on the matching blank. Lines are sgraffitoed into the dry powder to give texture to the background. This is the lower blank. The designed blank is placed over it, colored side down.

ONE COLOR ON ONE BLANK

Cut two blanks the same size. Draw the design on paper or cardboard and place a clean blank of glass over it. Paint in the design with squeegee oil following the drawn design. Place the blank on a paper towel. Sift powdered glass over the entire surface of the blank using a small sifter. Let the powder remain a few minutes to allow the oil to absorb as much of the powder as possible. Turn the blank on its side, tap off the excess powder on the paper towel. The powder remains on the blank where the oiled design was applied. Return the excess powder to its jar. Figs. 48 and 49.

TWO COLORS ON ONE BLANK

As explained in the chapter on Materials and How to Use Them, if two colors are to be applied on one blank using this method, paint in the oil for the darker color first. This is done so that if specks from the second color adhere to the first, the second color, being lighter, will not show up in the fired piece. Use the decorated glass as the upper blank.

It is practical to put the colors on the same blank when the colors do not overlap or when one does not surround the other. Figs. 50 to 57 "Iceland Poppies." Other examples, Figs. 58 and 59.

Fig. 50. "Iceland Poppies." The blank is placed over the drawn design and the lines of the darker color are oiled in.

Fig. 51. Opaque black powdered glass is sifted on the blank and the excess is tapped off.

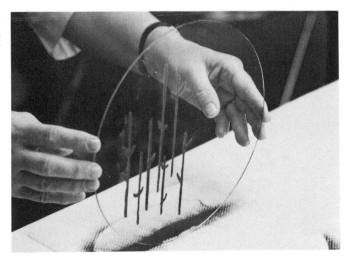

Fig. 52. The blank is returned to the design and the heads of the flowers are oiled in.

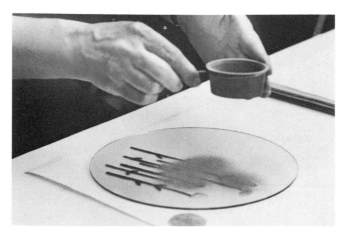

Fig. 53. Chinese red opaque powdered glass is sifted over the blank. To prevent any possibility of the second color affecting the first one, burn off the oil from the first color before proceeding to the second one.

Fig. 54. A layer of transparent clear ice is sifted on the matching blank, which is placed over the design. The outline of the design is sgraffitoed into the clear powder. The flower nearest the center has been omitted to prevent overlapping.

Fig. 55. The lower blank is placed on the prepared mold.

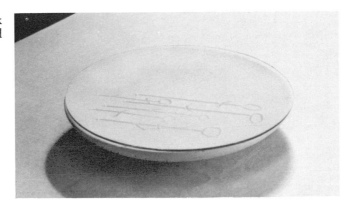

Fig. 56. After the oil is baked off the upper blank, it is placed over the lower blank with the design side down.

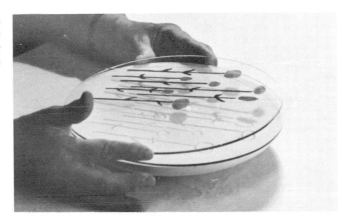

Fig. 57. "Iceland Poppies," the fired piece.

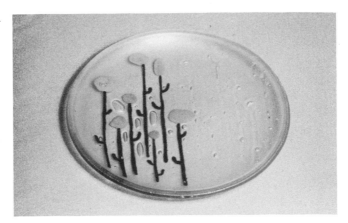

58

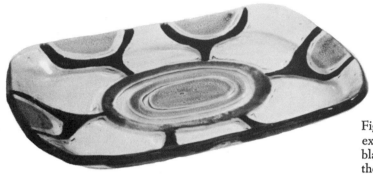

Fig. 58. "Scandinavia KRH." Another example of applying the colors to one blank. Three shades of blue were used, the darkest one first. Size 6½"x 9½". The designed blank was the upper one.

Fig. 59. "Black with White Triangles." The black was applied first and the oil burned off before adding the white to assure a strong black design. The triangles were then added using the first color as a guide.

TWO COLORS ON TWO BLANKS

The execution of the design "Berries and Leaves" is an example of where it is practical to apply part of the two-color design to each blank. Figs. 60 to 63.

It is necessary to reverse one of the parts of this design because, when assembling, the lower blank is turned up on the mold and the

Fig. 60. "Berries and Leaves." A blank was placed over the design and the outline of the leaves and berries was painted in with oil, the opaque Spruce Green powder was sifted over it, and the excess tapped off.

Fig. 61. The second blank was placed over the reversed design (see text). Opaque white powder was sifted over this oiled part of the design.

Fig. 62. After the oil was burned off, the two blanks were combined on the mold.

Fig. 63. "Berries and Leaves," the fired piece.

upper blank is placed down over it with the powdered or designed sides of the two blanks together. If the design is drawn on paper, place a piece of carbon paper under it with the carbon side up. Trace over the lines. Follow the pattern for one of the colors using the lines on the underside. If the design was first executed on cardboard, transfer it onto tracing paper and follow the lines on the "wrong" side for one of the colors.

Paint in the lines for one color of the design with squeegee oil. Then using the second blank, apply the oil for the other color, following the reverse design. When the two blanks are combined, one part of the design will mesh with the reverse part of the other.

"The Family," Figs. 64 to 68, shows another way of reversing the design for the second color and a more exact method than using a reverse pattern from paper since the thickness of the lines may vary when applying the oil.

Place a blank over the drawn design. Apply the oil for one of the colors. Sift the powder on the oiled blank and tap off the excess on a

Fig. 64. "The Family." The first blank is prepared as for "Berries and Leaves," Fig. 60. The powder is applied to the oiled lines and the excess tapped off.

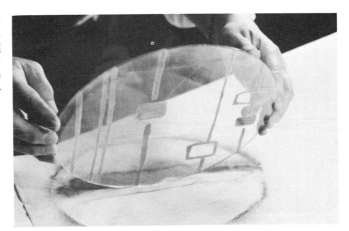

Fig. 65. The first blank is placed on a few scraps of glass with the prepared side down. The matching blank is placed on top and the oil for the second color is applied using the first blank as a guide.

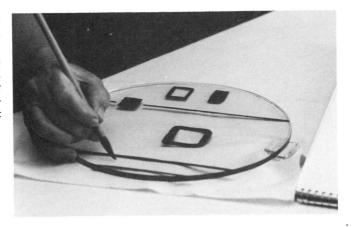

Fig. 66. The powder is sifted over the second blank and the excess is tapped off.

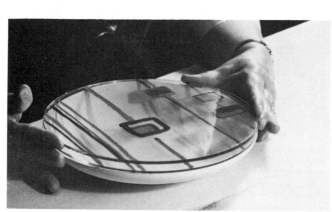

Fig. 67. After the oil has been baked off, the two blanks are assembled on the mold.

Fig. 68. "The Family," the fired piece.

Fig. 69. "Black and White Lines." The same technique is used as for "The Family," since the two colors are close together.

paper towel. Turn the decorated blank upside-down and rest it on small scraps of glass or any small objects that will keep the glass level and raised from the work surface. (The designed surface is on the underside.) If the glass scraps disturb a little of the design at the edges it can be touched up later.

Place the second blank on top of the first blank and oil in the part of the design for the second color using the lines of the first one as a guide. Remove the second blank to a paper towel and sift the second color over it. Tap off the excess and combine the blanks on top of the mold after burning off the oil in the oven.

The craftsman will have to determine which of these procedures is the more practical for the design to be executed.

Removing the Oil

Before two blanks can be combined and placed on a prepared mold for firing, the oil must be baked off. If the prepared blank or blanks are allowed to sit overnight and if their diameter does not exceed nine inches, burning off the oil in the oven may not be necessary. The use of heat is preferred because it can be done quickly in the kitchen oven or in a small table oven. It also prevents all possibility of having a small dark bubble become trapped in the middle of the piece. Another advantage of using an oven to burn off the oil is that correction and adjustment to the design can be made using a small tool without the risk of disturbing the rest of the design. The baking causes the powdered oil to become a soft crust.

Place a piece of aluminum foil on the oven rack to protect the blanks from any possible grease. Place the blanks on the foil in a cold oven. Turn on the oven. Turn it off when the temperature reaches 300 degrees F. Open the door and allow the oven to cool. Remove the blanks when they are cool enough to handle. This amount of heat has no effect on the glass.

Uses of Transparent Powders for Backgrounds

The following are optional steps. Transparent enamels and ices are adaptable to relate the background to the design for pieces that have an opaque colorant between laminated blanks, embossed pieces on top of laminated blanks, or pieces on the underside of them.

If the design covers only a small part of a blank, sift a light layer of transparent clear ice or glass flux over the matching blank before combining them. It gives a smoother appearance when fused.

A design related to the one that has been executed can be worked into the dry background powder using either a clear or transparent colored powder. Examples of this can be seen on "Eight Petals and Sixteen Leaves," Color Plate 1, and on "Three Trees," Color Plate 9. These plates are embossed with the sgraffito acting as part of the design in Color Plate 1 and as a suggestion of a shadow of the pieces in Color Plate 9.

Another example is shown in Fig. 57, "Iceland Poppies." The transparent clear sgraffitoed design is the same as the opaque design applied to one side.

"Twice Twelve," Fig. 106, shows the transparent colored background sgraffitoed to relate to the shape of the pieces of glass which have been fused to the underside.

Assembly Before Firing

If a top-loading kiln is used, the molds may be placed in the kiln and the glass parts assembled in the kiln. Place the prepared mold, coated with a separating powder, on the kiln shelf. Then put the designed blank on the mold and if it is to be laminated, cover with a blank the same size. If the design has been applied to two blanks, hold the upper over the lower one to determine the exact position to have the parts of the design mesh. Do not allow the two to touch until the proper placement is determined. Raise the upper blank if it is necessary to correct the positioning after placing it. Do not turn the upper blank while it is in contact with the lower one.

If small pieces are to be embossed, they may be glued on the blank with Elmer's glue before the blank is placed on the mold. This particular glue burns out in the firing, leaving no residue.

Sgraffito

Sgraffito, in Italian, means scratch. It is a method used in decorating many craft media.

DRY POWDER

Sift a thin even layer of opaque powdered glass or enice over the entire blank. The design is then executed by removing some of the powder or scratching into it. Fig. 70.

If the layer of powder is light in color and thin enough, the guide

Fig. 70. "The Volley-ball." A light coating of opaque Princeton orange powdered glass is sifted on a blank and placed on a decorating wheel over a paper towel.

lines of a design worked out on paper will show through. A felt pen with a thin point is a good drawing instrument for a design that will be used under the powder. A lamp under a sheet of glass that is suspended at its sides will assist in following the lines of the design if dark powders are applied to the blank.

A slant-edged tool was used to form the lines in "Volleyball," Fig. 71. The lines that extend to the edge permit air to escape and prevent unwanted bubbles that might otherwise be trapped. Fig. 72.

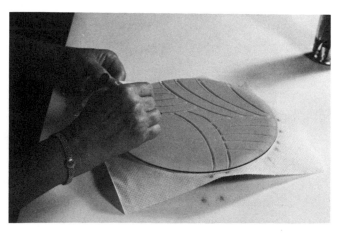

Fig. 71. The powder is removed to create the design. The decorated blank is placed on the prepared mold and a clear blank is positioned on top.

Fig. 72. "The Volley-
ball," the fired piece.

Fig. 73. "S and a Half."
This twelve-inch diam-
eter white plate had a
very light application of
opaque powder, thus the
transparency of the glass
is not lost. The tech-
nique used is the same
as for "Volleyball," Fig.
70.

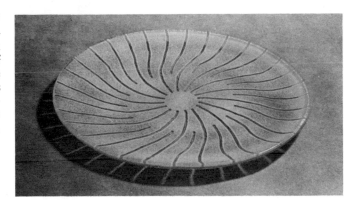

Fig. 74. "Many Points,"
another example where
the powder is removed
to create the design.
Two fifteen-inch diam-
eter blanks are sgraffi-
toed, using Diagram 2
then sprayed and com-
bined to form the design.
The fired piece may be
seen in Color Plate 2.

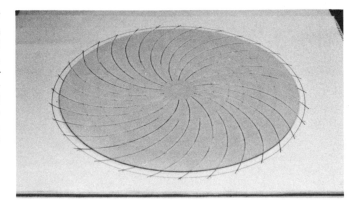

A brush with stiff plastic bristles is the tool used to make the "Swirls" design. Start in the center of a blank that has a layer of powder sifted on it, and disturb the powder with a circular motion, in the center first. Lift the brush and work in the same manner around the blank ending up at the edge of the glass for each swirl. This will get rid of some of the powder and thus open up the design. Opaque powder is recommended using a light layer. Figs. 75 and 76.

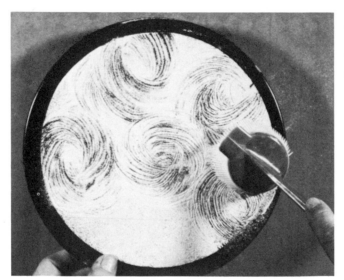

Fig. 75. "Swirls." The blank was prepared in the same way as for "Volleyball," using opaque white powder (see text).

Fig. 76. "Swirls," the fired piece.

Fig. 77. "Ringlets." The blank was prepared in the same way as for "The Volleyball." An opalescent powder was used.

Fig. 78. "Ringlets," the fired piece.

The design for "Ringlets" was achieved by disturbing the powder without getting rid of any of it. Using a slant edged tool, carve the design into the powder. When an even light coating of opaque powder is applied and the sgraffitoed lines are thin, unwanted bubbles will not be trapped. The thin trail of bubbles resulting from the sgraffitoed lines will enhance the design. Figs. 77 and 78.

A COATING OF OIL ON A BLANK

This technique may be used if a sprayer is not available. Apply a coating of squeegee oil over an entire blank. Put a blank the same size on top of the oiled blank and move it in a circular motion. This will smooth the oil that was applied to the blank, erasing the brush marks, and will put an even coating of oil on the other blank. If two projects are planned or if powdered glass is needed on both blanks, this coats two blanks at a time. Sift the powder over the oiled blank or blanks. Tap off the excess. Bake off the oil in an oven, and scratch in the design. A coating of transparent clear ice or other flux is sifted on top of an opaque powder if the piece is not to be laminated. Remove the oil from the unpowdered blank if it is to be used to cover a prepared blank.

This method of powder application is used also when the opaque powder is to be fired on the underside of the blank. In other words, the powder is next to the mold. No transparent clear ice is added nor is flux sifted over the opaque coating.

The Combination of Embossing and Sgraffito

The following combines embossing and sgraffito, two techniques that complement each other. An example of this is illustrated in Figs. 79 to 82, "Eight Petals and Sixteen Leaves."

Fig. 79. "Eight Petals and Sixteen Leaves." A twelve-inch blank is placed over the diagram. Either transparent clear or colored powder is sifted over the blank in an even layer and slightly heavier in the center.

Fig. 80. Using a tool, remove the powder following the scallops on Diagram 1.

Fig. 81. The sgraffitoed blank is placed on the mold and a matching blank is placed on top before adding the pieces to be embossed.

Fig. 82. Or the upper blank may be placed over the diagram and the pieces positioned for embossing. If the pieces are glued in place on the upper blank, it is important that the diagram be accurately drawn. Align the two blanks. The fired piece may be seen in Color Plate 1.

Cut two blanks twelve inches in diameter. Draw a leaf and a petal on paper to be used as a pattern for cutting the pieces to be embossed. There should be good contrast between their sizes. Then draw guide lines on the glass to identify the points where the scoring will intersect and give uniformity to the pieces. See chapter "Cutting Glass," Fig. 31.

If thin sharp pinpoints remain at the ends of the pieces, snip them with wide-nosed pliers before applying the colorant. These small pieces are to be picked up at their points after the powder has been applied.

Sift a thin layer of transparent or opaque powder or an ice over the lower blank. Apply powder as evenly as possible, adding a slightly heavier amount in the center. As mentioned before, the fusing will take place first where the powder is thicker. Treating the center in this manner assures the elimination of an air bubble from being trapped in the middle. A thin application of opaque should be used. A little more ice is needed than opaque to give color to this background and an additional amount of transparent if it is to be the background. Transparent clear powder will give a colorless background but the sgraffitoed lines will show.

To sgraffito the design, remove the powder that is applied to the blank with a tool following the scallops, Fig. 80. These lines are primarily a part of the design but by carrying them to the edge of the blank they serve as an escape route for air which might otherwise be trapped. The scratched-in design also is a guide for placing the embossed pieces with accuracy.

Coat the petals and leaves with oil before sifting the dry powder on them to attain an even coating. If preferred, liquid colorants may be applied. When oil has been used on pieces that are exposed, it is not necessary to burn it off or let it dry, as it will evaporate during the early stages of firing. If an opaque powder is used, top the pieces with transparent clear ice or a flux.

Sift a separator on the mold. Place the sgraffitoed blank on the mold. Place the pieces to be embossed around the upper blank, using the paper design as a guide. A drop of Elmer's glue on the underside of each piece will keep them in place. An accurate placement of the pieces can be made by putting the upper blank over the lower one and then assembling the embossed pieces, Figs. 81 and 82. The fired piece is shown in color in Color Plate 1.

Designing With Bubbles

Up to now ways of preventing the formation of bubbles in a design have been pointed out. It is possible to create bubbles and predetermine the size, shape, and placement of them. The following techniques are presented whereby bubbles are deliberately created to form the design.

It is essential to make up sheets of lines on heavy paper or cardboard for use in developing patterns in which there are parallel lines as well as for planned bubbles. These guide sheets also are used under glass for cutting glass strips, squares, and rectangles. Make up a separate sheet for lines ⅜, ½, etc., inches apart. Draw the lines with a fine-pointed, black, felt pen to strengthen the visibility of the lines when the blank is coated with powdered glass.

SINGLE BUBBLES

Painting with oil as described in this chapter is the procedure for bubbles. A bubble is accomplished by trapping air within a small area surrounded by powdered glass. The powder becomes soft and fuses before the glass starts to bend and before two pieces of glass fuse to each other.

If perfect squares and bubbles equal in size are desired, oil in the lines the same width and the same distance apart on each of two blanks of equal size. Sift the powder over the blanks, tap off the excess and burn off the oil in the usual manner. Then scratch off any irregularities. As mentioned before, when an oiled design has been placed in a cold oven and heated to 300 degrees F. the powder becomes a soft crust. This simplifies making corrections, which are usually needed where straight lines are involved.

Place the lower blank on the prepared mold and cover with the upper blank, with the lines at right angles to the lines on the lower blank, the powdered glass on the two blanks touching. If it is necessary to correct the position, lift the upper blank and adjust the angle while holding it above the lower blank before replacing it. Figs. 83 to 89.

Fig. 83. "Single Bubbles." Oil is applied following the diagram of lines.

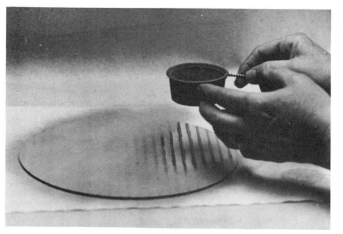

Fig. 84. Transparent colored powder is sifted over the lines, in this case, Evergreen.

Fig. 85. The excess is tapped off. Another blank is prepared in the same way as the first and the oil is burned off both.

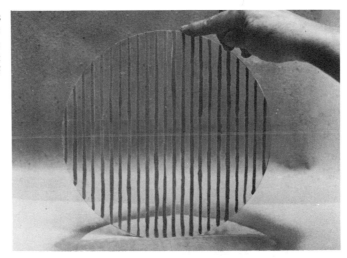

Fig. 86. Scratch off any irregularities from the crust formed by burning off the oil.

Fig. 87. One blank is placed on the prepared mold.

Fig. 88. The second blank is positioned over the lower blank with the lines at right angles to each other.

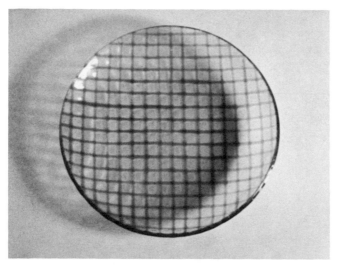

Fig. 89. "Single Bubbles," the fired piece. The lines are ½ inch apart.

DOUBLING THE BUBBLES

Twice as many bubbles as single bubbles may be achieved using the same diagram. This method is actually the combination of sgraffito and the use of oil with the powdered glass.

Place a blank over the selected diagram of lines and oil in the lines. Set the blank on a paper towel. Sift on either an ice or a transparent powdered glass. Tap off the excess, bake off the oil, and correct the irregularities. This is the upper blank.

For the lower blank, sift an even layer of powder on another blank the same size. The powder may be the same color as the upper blank or a contrasting one. Use a fairly heavy coating. A thin layer will result in very small bubbles. Control the size according to the plan chosen. If the coating is too heavy the sgraffitoed lines will tend to close up when assembled with the upper blank. A few experiments will help determine how much powder is required to give the desired effect.

Transparent powders and ices reveal the bubbles more effectively than opaque powders. A combination of two colors will give a hint of a third color where they intersect.

To duplicate a piece using the same color combination, it is important that the color of the upper and lower blanks be in the same order. By reversing the colors of the blanks a different value of the colors will result.

If a dark powder or a heavier coating of any powder is used on the lower blank, it will be difficult to follow the guide lines of the diagram. Use a ruler to make a light depression in the powder at each line of the diagram. The extension of the lines beyond the blank on the diagram will be the guide.

Remove the powder using a tool to sgraffito thin lines in the soft powder. This is the lower blank. Top it with the blank of oiled lines. An oblong bubble will be where the line is sgraffitoed and a round one will be "trapped" with air that is in the dry powder. Figs. 90 to 94.

RANDOM BUBBLES

Random bubbles result when ⅛ teaspoon of baking soda is added to one tablespoon of powdered glass. Sift an even thin layer of the mixture on a blank. Cover with a matching blank. In Fig. 95 HFT-green

Fig. 90. "Double Bubbles." Follow the step-by-step preparation for a blank of single bubbles, which will be the upper blank for double bubbles. The lower blank is placed over the diagram of lines used for the upper blank. Using either the same transparent powder for this blank or a contrasting one, sift an even coating of powder over it. (See text for application.) Remove a thin line of powder at each line.

Fig. 91. If a heavy coating of powder is applied or if the color is dark, making it hard to follow the lines, use a ruler to make a light depression at each line as a guide.

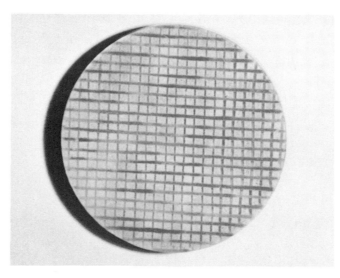

Fig. 92. Place the un-oiled blank on a prepared mold and position the lines of the upper blank at right angles to the lower one. Where the thin open space shows through, there will be a long thin bubble. Where the heavy powder is squared by the oiled lines there will be a round bubble. Bluebell Blue was applied on the lower blank and Lawn Green on the upper one.

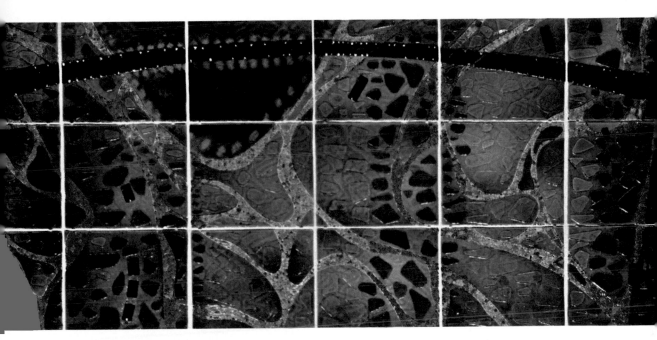

Color Plate 12. Fused glass mural in the Rivers Suite of the Pittsburgh Hilton Hotel. Each panel is four feet by ten feet. The theme is the conjunction of the two rivers to form the Ohio at Pittsburgh. The sections of this panel are made up of fused stained glass and attached to an opaque white wall with an adhesive. By R. B. Beaman.

Color Plate 13. "The Gizmo." Welding rods were covered with copper foil. Solder was applied to the foil. The stained glass pieces have came around them with half of the double channel removed. The came is attached to the prepared welding rods with solder. The base is four by four inch lumber painted black.

Color Plate 14. "Fish and Fowl."

Color Plate 15. Stained glass panel by John Buescher, a student at the University of Virginia.

Color Plate 16. The "Chess Set" by Bette Bartelmes in the School of Graduate Studies at the University of Michigan.

Color Plate 17. "The Cross."

Color Plate 18. "Bottle People" by Ruth Walters. Transparent Glass Stains were dripped into each large bottle and flakes of mica were added. The necks of small bottles (faces) were inserted in the necks of the larger ones. Chips of glass were used for the features on the faces. These were fired flat on a kiln shelf. Bottle labels were glued to a wooden backing. The fired "people" and stained glass tesserae were glued over the labels and a coating of clear plastic was poured over the framed assemblage.

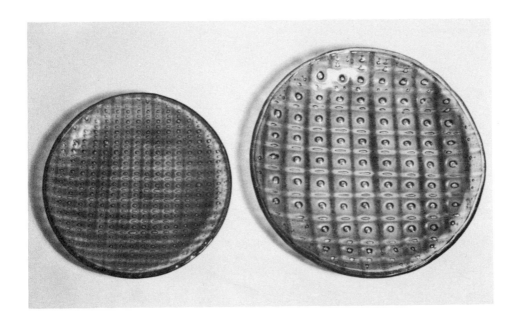

Fig. 93. "Double Bubbles." The lines of the seven-inch diameter piece are ⅜ inch apart. The lines of the 9½-inch diameter piece are ¾ inch apart.

Fig. 94. "Double Bubbles." The lines are one-half inch apart on this 15-inch plate.

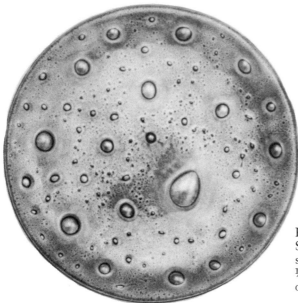

Fig. 95. Random bubbles. "Moon Surface," the fired piece. One tablespoon of HFT-green was mixed with ⅛ teaspoon of baking soda and sifted on the lower blank.

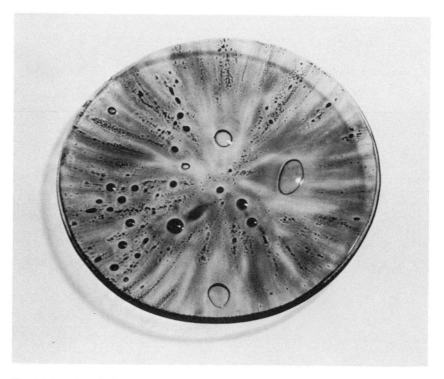

Fig. 96. Random bubbles. "Sun Rays." Finely ground opaque enamel was mixed with oil and one-half teaspoon baking soda added. The oil was burned off in the oven before laminating.

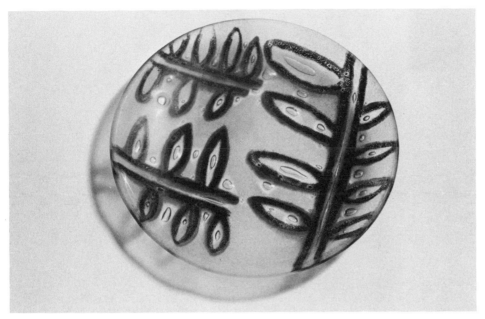

Fig. 97. Unplanned bubbles. "Three Branches" is an example of bubbles of trapped air which result from surrounding an open area with powder. It is known that bubbles will result but the arrangement is affected by the thickness of the lines and their distances apart. A transparent turquoise powder was sifted on the lower blank. Opaque brown was used on the designed blank.

was used. A thin film of opaque powder will achieve the same results. HFT-yellow fractures.

UNPLANNED BUBBLES

A bubble will result in any small space completely surrounded by powdered glass, oiled or not. These are characteristic of slumped glass and give interest to the finished piece. Bubbles that are very large are undesirable since the pressure inside may cause a fracture and because they may dominate the design. Fig. 97.

Embossed Designs on Plate Glass

The surface of most plate glass crystalizes in the firing. The glass takes on a frosted appearance. This background gives good contrast to

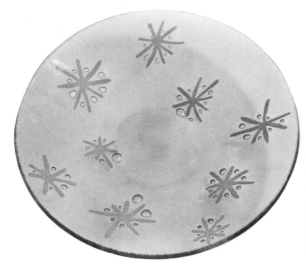

Fig. 98. Unplanned bubbles. "Stars." The lower blank of this fifteen-inch diameter bowl has a red ice background. This color fires to an almost transparent rose. The stars were applied with oil and a white opaque powder was sifted over them.

the shiny embossed pieces. However, if overfired, the surface will be rough. If the frosting is to be eliminated, after the embossed pieces have been placed on a plate glass blank, sift a light layer of transparent clear ice over the entire surface. Some glass fluxes show little lines on plate glass. A transparent glass glaze liquid may be painted on before adding the embossed pieces.

Apply a small amount of Elmer's glue to the pieces before placing them on a blank. Or the blank may be positioned on a prepared mold and the embossed pieces placed directly on the blank without the use of glue. This is recommended if a top-loading kiln is used and it is located near the work area. The advantage of not using glue is that it is easier to change the position of a piece, if desired, after placements have been made. Figs. 99 to 101.

The Design on the Underside

PLATE GLASS

The reverse of embossing pieces on top of plate glass to create a design is to place the cut-out pieces of glass in the bottom of the mold

Fig. 99. "One Flower." Oil is applied to the pieces to be embossed to assure an even coating of the powder which is sifted on them.

Fig. 100. The pieces are positioned on the plate glass blank on the mold.

Fig. 101. "One Flower," the fired piece.

and place the blank on top. By this procedure, the surface of the finished piece is smooth although it is slightly raised where the design has fused to the underside.

Cut out pieces to be used for the design. Lightly oil the pieces and sift powdered glass, usually opaque, over them. Because they will be covered, it is necessary to bake off the oil from the pieces before placing them in the bottom of the mold.

Sift the separating powder on the mold or use a mold which has been prepared with a separating powder in paste form. Place the prepared pieces in the bottom of the mold. They should be on the flat part or floor of the mold. If they are arranged on the part of the mold that has a slight curve, it will not impair the finished piece.

It is difficult to put pieces in place without disturbing the dry separator. However, a slight disturbance will not impair the separation of the glass from the mold. In executing this design technique, if the paste separator is applied and the surface smoothed to eliminate all grooves and marks, fire without the addition of the dry separator if it presents a problem when placing the pieces in the floor of the mold.

Apply a thin film of transparent clear ice on the plate glass blank or use a flux that has been pretested for plate glass to assure compatibility. It is a matter of preference as to which coating is used. Place the prepared blank on top of the mold and fire according to the firing schedule. Fig. 102.

LAMINATED SINGLE- AND DOUBLE-STRENGTH GLASS

The same technique as with plate glass is used when the designed pieces are placed in the bottom of a mold and topped with two blanks of single- or double-strength glass. Laminated blanks give the opportunity to work a simple related design between the blanks. In "Multicolored Hard Edge," by separating the pieces that comprise the circle and handling each individually when applying the colorants, a clear hard-edge was effected.

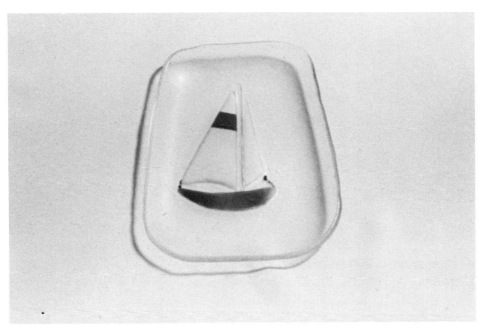

Fig. 102. "Sailboat," opaque blue boat with white sails and red stripe.

The pieces were oiled, and the opaque powder sifted on and the oil burned off. If preferred, the pieces may be placed in the bottom of the mold and burned off in the kiln. A thin layer of opaque cream colored powder was sifted on the outer rim of the lower blank, forming a two-inch border with the four and one-half inch diameter design on the underside in the center when fired. The powder was removed in eight equidistant lines to the edge of the piece. Here again, as in the "Sailboat," Fig. 102, the inside of the finished piece is smooth. To eliminate the possibility of trapping air in the middle of the blanks, transparent ice was sifted in the center of the lower blank. Figs. 103 to 105.

Another example of laminated pieces with the small cut pieces on the underside is "Twice Twelve," Fig. 106. The slight curve of the mold on which some of the small pieces were placed did not have an adverse effect upon the finished piece.

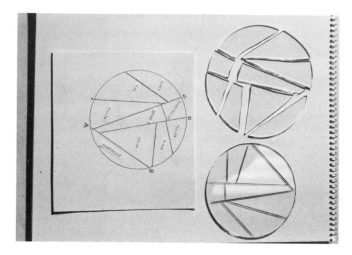

Fig. 103. "Multicolored Hard Edge," showing the detail for planning and cutting the pieces. Line "A" to "B" must be cut first.

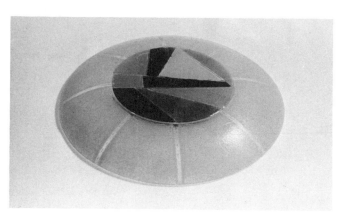

Fig. 104. The underside of the bowl after firing.

Fig. 105. "Multicolored Hard Edge," the fired piece.

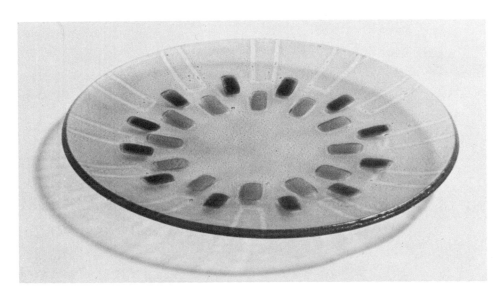

Fig. 106. "Twice Twelve," another example of firing on the underside. The sgraffitoed transparent pale green powder laminated between the blanks gives a related background for the opaque deep blue and light green pieces.

Fig. 107. "Sunflower." The center is oiled in, Princeton orange opaque powder sifted over it, and the excess tapped off. Protect the orange with a circle of glass or cardboard when applying the opaque yellow leaves. Sift HFT-yellow over the entire plate glass blank and top with a bare minimum of transparent clear ice or a flux.

THREE BLANKS

Lines were applied with oil following the paper design on two blanks. Opaque powder was sifted over the lines and the excess tapped off. After the oil was burned off, a light sifting of the same color opaque enamel was applied in the center of each prepared blank. Delft Blue and white or Pea Green and white are good combinations. The Delft Blue blank was placed on the mold with the powder side up. Then the white

Fig. 108. A light sifting of powder is applied to the center of each prepared blank.

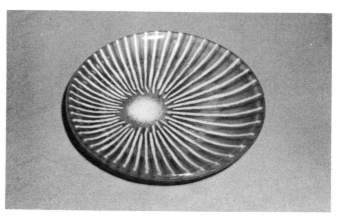

Fig. 109. "Looking at a Dome from an Angle," the fired piece.

blank was placed on top of the lowest blank with the powder side up and the lines of the middle blank running through the spaces between the blue lines. A clear blank topped the other two. Figs. 108 and 109.

Embossed Panels

Single-strength glass pieces are decorated with opaque powdered glass and fired on double-strength glass panels. After the pieces are placed, the entire blanks are coated with a light sifting of transparent clear ice. They may be cut to fit a windowpane and held in place with colored cloth tape. Also, they may be backed with colored paper and hung in a child's room using transparent corner-type hangers. Fig. 110.

A Happening

The influence of Jackson Pollack was the cause of "The Happening." Squeegee oil was spattered on a fifteen-inch diameter blank with a small Japanese brush. The spattering was washed off several times before the desired distribution of oil was achieved. Beginning with the darkest color first, opaque powder was sifted on selected areas of the blank. None of the powder was tapped off until the blank was completely covered with all the colors. After the excess was tapped off, the oil was burned off in an oven. For pieces made from plate glass, transparent clear ice or a flux would have to be sifted on top without burning off the oil. Figs. 111 and 112. Color Plate 7 shows the fired piece in color.

Transparent Plate Glass With Color

Plate glass is available in one-quarter inch thick sheets and is tinted gray and bronze. Fig. 113 has been cut to fit the mold, and to prevent the surface from becoming frosted, has a sifting of transparent clear ice on it. The blank should be cut from a sheet allowing at least a one inch margin to accomplish a smooth cleavage.

Fig. 110. "Three Embossed Panes." Single-strength pieces are embossed on double-strength glass. They may be made to fit a windowpane and held in place with colored cloth tape. Or they may be backed with colored paper and hung in a child's room using transparent corner-type hangers.

Fig. 111. The squeegee oil was spattered on the blank in designing "The Happening."

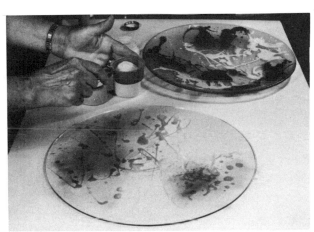

Fig. 112. Opaque powdered glass of selected colors was sifted over the blank before lifting it to tap off the excess. The fired piece may be seen in Color Plate 7.

Fig. 113. "Unadorned." The two ashtrays are made from colored plate glass. The round one is gray and the square one is bronze tone. A square of glass was placed in the bottom of the mold and a square blank cut to fit the mold was placed on top. No colorant was added. A light coating of clear transparent ice was sifted over each piece to prevent frosting.

7

Silk Screen Printing on Glass

The silk screen printing process is especially useful when duplicate items, such as sets of dessert plates, are desired. Using this process obviously takes away from the individuality that results when pieces are prepared by hand. But it has its place because of its practicality on otherwise time-consuming projects.

The various methods of applying the design to the screen are the same for glass as for fabrics, greeting cards, posters, and ceramics. Regardless of which procedure is selected, the silk is blocked out except where the colorant will print on the glass. The open areas of the silk become the design.

The screen will last for years if it is treated with care. The colorant should be cleaned off thoroughly when the printing has been completed. The design may be left on the screen and used again at a later date.

The dimensions given are for a screen that can accommodate a design up to nine inches square. The figures in parentheses are for a screen for designs up to twelve inches square. The actual size of the silk is 18″ × 18″ (21″ × 21″). The size of the exposed silk is 10½″ × 10½″ (13½″ × 13½″), which leaves a ¾-inch margin when the largest dimension is used. This margin is necessary for two reasons. If the design is placed too close to the tape on the screen the printing may be impaired because the stiff tape prevents proper contact with the glass blank. In addition, when the colorant is poured onto the taped border, colorant might seep through if it is too close to the open area of the silk.

Small screens naturally require less preparation but there is no minimum to the size design that can be applied on a large screen. If a large amount of work is planned that requires only a small printing area, it is practical to make a small screen for easy handling and cleaning.

The wood framing is a standard size available at the lumber yard. If the width of the wood can be stripped down, it would be better so that shorter nails may be used, thus preventing the possibility of splitting the wood. The size of 1×2 inch lumber is actually ¾×1⅝ inches. This can be trimmed to measure ¾×1¼ inches. Silk screen silk is usually 40 inches wide.

If materials required for making a screen are not available locally, they may be ordered by mail from the craft supply houses listed in Sources of Materials and Supplies.

Materials needed are:

> 12 XX silk screen silk, 18 inches square (20×21)
> Roll of gummed mailing tape
> 1×2 inch lumber, 8 feet (9 feet)
> Stapling gun preferably or small tacks
> Thick tempered masonite, 21″×18″ (24″×21″)
> 2 pin hinges (one set)
> Clear shellac and paint brush
> Rubber-edged squeegee, 11½ inches long (14½ inches)
> Nails, 8 or more two-inch finishing nails

Making the Screen

Cut two pieces of wood 17 inches long (20″) and two pieces 14½ inches long (17″). Join the pieces at each end with two nails so that the frame will measure approximately 17″×17″ (20″×20″) around the outer edge of the wood. This is the simplest method of joining although mitering the corners is neater. The gummed paper will strengthen the joints and mitering is not a necessity. If the corners are mitered, the length of each piece of wood before mitering would be a minimum of 18 inches (21″).

Instead of cutting the silk, tear it to size. Although this is very fine material, aligning the weave is helpful when applying the design with a liquid, especially when a very fine-line detailed design is being put on the screen. Less intricate designs would not be affected.

The silk is stapled near the outer edge of the frame. It is very important that the silk be taut. Possibly some staples may have to be removed and replaced if puckers show up, but this should not be done until the initial stapling is completed.

Start stapling at the center on one side. Then place a few staples first on one side of the center then on the other side in a herringbone pattern. Alternate until there is about one inch left to be stapled at each corner of the first side. All corners will be done last. When stapling pull the silk as tight as possible in the direction you are stapling, first from one end and then the other on the same side. Do not pull across the frame for the first side. Next, start stapling at the center of the opposite side,

Fig. 114. The silk is stapled to the frame.

pulling across the frame. As the stapling progresses along this side, pull the silk toward the end you are working, in addition to pulling across the frame. The third side is stapled starting from the center and working from side to side toward the corners. Pull the silk taut from side to side only. Pull in both directions, across and side to side, when stapling the fourth side. Fig. 114. Staple the corners last. Pull out staples wherever there are any puckers and re-staple. Trim off the excess silk so that the material is the size of the outer edges of the frame.

Measure 1¾ inches from the inside of the frame and draw lines with a soft pencil on the silk at all four sides. These are guide lines for placing the gummed tape. Beginning at the drawn lines, moisten and place tape along these lines. Then build up tape to cover the wood frame with one or two layers of tape, overlapping the edges on both sides of the frame. It will be necessary to do a little snipping and fitting at the inside corners. When it is thoroughly dry, shellac the tape, being careful not to get any on the exposed silk. A second coat of shellac is not necessary but will hold up longer. After the shellac is completely dry, wet the silk thoroughly and let dry. The screen is now ready to have the design applied.

Nail a strip of wood the thickness of the taped screen plus the thickness of a piece of double-strength glass, which is ⅛ inch, to the smooth side of the masonite. This bar can be the same 1 by 2 inch lumber with a thin strip of wood under it. If available, a ⅞-inch thick strip of wood is needed. The length is 21 inches (24″). The screen will overlap the masonite by about one inch so that the screen may be lifted easily during printing.

Screw the pin hinges to the bar and at the top of the screen. Screw a small piece of wood about six inches long and no thicker than the frame to one side of the screen. The screw is about five inches from the end of the strip and the end of the screen as well. This is a stilt to keep the screen raised when placing the glass blanks during the printing process. Fig. 123.

Applying the Design

USING A LIQUID

Work out the design on paper. The drawn design is placed under the silk screen and penciled in on the silk. Do not use a very sharp pencil or press hard enough to damage the silk.

Maskoid is one of the liquids that can be used to apply the design. It is a rubber-base material which can be removed from the screen by rubbing with the finger or by using a pencil eraser. Tusche is another liquid and is easy to control, especially for a design with fine detail. It is removable from the screen with varsol.

Do not allow the underside of the screen to touch the table or work area when applying the design because wherever it touches the application will not be solid.

Following the penciled lines, paint the design on the screen with the liquid, Fig. 115. Check the design by holding the screen up to the light. Touch up any places where the light leaks through. If lines are left out of the design and the blockout is applied, it is difficult to open up the screen afterward. However, if too much liquid has been applied, coat the screen with the blockout, remove the liquid and touch up these

Fig. 115. The design is painted with tusche following the penciled lines.

places using a paint brush and blockout. This is done when a thick line is to be made thinner.

USING THE BLOCKOUT

When the liquid, maskoid or tusche, is thoroughly dry the blockout is squeegeed on. LePage's Strength Glue, Naz Dar's Watermask, or Southwestern Process' Watersol may be used. The glue takes quite a while to dry and cannot be used in damp hot weather whereas the others mentioned dry in about ten minutes. They were developed for this use. None of the blockouts will stick to the liquid used to apply the design.

Place four small blocks of wood, one inch high, under the screen at the four corners to raise the screen to prevent the underside of the

Fig. 116. Pouring the blockout on the screen.

silk from touching the table or work area. If this should happen, wash the screen with water and start again. Pour enough blockout at one end of the screen to coat it. Fig. 116. Do not allow the blockout to blot on the silk. Use a squeegee that is a size large enough to overlap the silk; that is, if the silk measures 10½ inches, an 11½-inch squeegee is used. Pull the blockout down toward you from the upper end of the screen where

Fig. 117. Coating the screen with blockout.

the blockout was poured. This should give an even, thin coating to the screen. Fig. 117.

If necessary, apply again. It is better to have two thin coatings than one that is too heavy. The reason for a second coating would be if little pinhole leaks show up when checking the screen by holding it up to the light after the blockout is dry. If there are only a few pinholes they may be touched up by applying blockout with a brush.

Immediately upon pulling the blockout over the screen, put the squeegee down, pick up the screen and pour off any excess blockout. Fig. 118. Care must be taken to avoid having the screen touch the table before

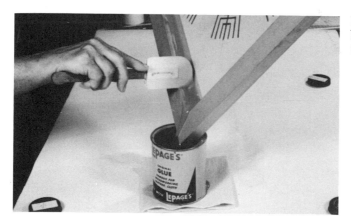

Fig. 118. The excess blockout is returned to the can.

it is dry. Using a wet paper towel, wipe the excess from the tape on the four sides without disturbing any of the blockout on the silk. Keep the container with the blockout closed when not in use. If it thickens, thin it with water.

After the blockout has dried, remove the liquid that was used to apply the design. The screen is now clean where the design was applied, thus opening the silk to allow the colorant to go through when printing. Actually, the prepared screen is now a stencil.

Before printing, inspect the screen. If some of the liquid used to apply the design is still on the screen, and it is not removable with an eraser or varsol (depending upon which liquid was used) lightly scratch it with your fingernail, since it is possible that a bit of the blockout has stuck to the design. If the silk is opened up beyond the design, this is the time to make corrections by painting it in with blockout.

Preparing for Printing

Attach the screen to the masonite backing using the pin hinges. Using the glass blank on which the printing is to be done, trace around it on bristol board or other type of stiff board and cut out the shape. The thickness of the board will depend upon the thickness of the glass. This board frames the blank to prevent the edge of the glass from being pressed against the silk while printing. The minimum size of the board should be the size of the exposed silk plus a 1½-inch border. For the screen described a 13 × 13 inch piece would be used.

If the design does not come near the edge of the blank, cut a piece of freezer paper or heavy wrapping paper the size of the screen and cut out a hole smaller than the blank but larger than the design to be printed. Tape it to the underside of the screen positioning it to the design on the silk. This prevents the glass from coming in contact with the silk and eliminates the need of the bristol board.

Attach a piece of paper to the masonite with masking tape. Draw the outline of the blank on the paper after positioning it to the design on the

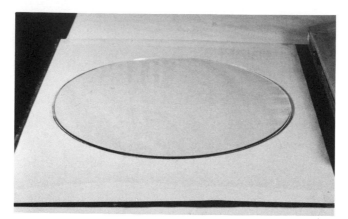

Fig. 119. The blank is lined up with the design on the screen and outlined with a pencil.

Fig. 120. The cut out stiff board surrounds the blank to protect the silk from the edges of the glass.

screen. This is the guide when feeding the blanks to be printed. Place a blank in position, then the board, and now rest the screen on the blank. Figs. 119 and 120.

Preparing the Colorant

Versa colors for silk screen printing have an iridescent appearance when fired. If used for laminating, the printed blank must first be fired flat to 500 degrees F. to burn off whatever becomes trapped in the center of the fired piece, causing a dark area. It may be used successfully if not laminated without prefiring. There are other glazes available for silk screen use.

Thompson's High Fire Opaque series may be used by mixing the dry powder with squeegee oil. If the blockout is water base, the colorant should not be water base as it would disintegrate the blockout. If film is used to apply the design (not described in this text) it is water resistant and can be used with this High Fire (HF) series mixed with water.

MIXING

Versa colors are available in liquid form and can be used from the jar. The HF powders are mixed by adding enough squeegee oil to give them the consistency of thick syrup. Mix thoroughly to remove all granules. The amount of the mixture needed will depend upon the size of the design and the number of prints to be made. Twelve prints were made using one-half cup of red Versa color for "Candlelight," Color Plate 8.

The mixture must be thick but must flow. If it is too thin, the coating will look weak and may run on the glass beyond the design. Any colorant left over may be used later. Store in a jar with a tight lid.

Printing the Design

Pour the colorant on the tape at one end of the screen. Pull it over the screen with the squeegee with one firm pull, holding the squeegee at an angle so that only the sharp edge of the squeegee is touching the silk. Using the small stilt which is screwed to the side of the screen, suspend the screen, remove the board and the printed blank. Put the next blank in place following the circle drawn on the paper, replace the board and continue printing. Because this design was large for the screen the squeegee was pulled across the screen twice for each printing. Figs. 121-123.

The number of colorants available for silk screen printing on glass are limited. Versa colors may be mixed to get any color desired. Any

Fig. 121. The paint is poured on the screen.

Fig. 122. The paint is squeegeed across the screen.

Fig. 123. Remove the stiff board and then the printed blank. The laminated fired piece is shown in Color Plate 8.

opaque powdered glass may be sifted on top of the printed design to change the original color while it is still wet. Sift powder over the printed design and tap off the excess. If the piece is not to be laminated, sift a light dusting over the powder using transparent clear ice or a clear flux.

As explained in the chapter Laminating and Decorating Glass, if the oiled design is to be covered with another blank, the oil must first be burned off. Place the printed blank in a cold oven and heat to 350 degrees F. Since an excessive amount of oil has been used in comparison with that in the earlier chapter, allow the glass to remain at 350 degrees for ten minutes before turning off the oven. Remove when cool enough to handle.

Cleaning the Screen

When the printing is completed, remove the pins from the hinges and place the screen on a few layers of newspaper. After wiping off the excess colorant with a paper towel, pour varsol over the screen and wipe off with a paper towel and then with a clean cloth for final cleaning. Clean the squeegee with varsol. The screen may be put away to print the same design another time or it may be washed with water to remove the blockout.

Printing Two Colors on One Blank

It is practical, but not necessary, to have two screens exactly the same size if a large amount of printing with two colors is planned. Only one backing made of masonite is needed. The pin hinges are screwed on both screens in the same position. Only half of one of the sets is used since they are both pinned into the same part of the hinge that is screwed on the wooden strip on the backing. To assure correct registration, apply both parts of the design in the same position on both screens. If registration is not exact, adjust the paper guide that has been taped to the masonite.

When two colors are printed on one blank, the darker color is printed first and, if the HF series is used, the oil is burned off before replacing it for the second color. If Versa colors are used, they may be placed in the oven for a few minutes to dry or allowed to dry naturally, which takes a very short time. The shiny surface dulls and will not be disturbed when printing over it.

If only one screen is used, the screen is prepared for the first color, the blank is printed, the colorant is removed, the screen is washed with water and the design for the second part is applied.

A simpler procedure is possible when the two colors in the design do not touch. The entire design is applied to the screen. Using two pieces of freezer paper the size of the screen, trace the design on the paper, shiny side down, using carbon paper to obtain two exact copies. Cut out the part for the first color from one copy and the part for the second color from the other copy. Tape one paper to the underside of the screen. The paper will serve as an additional blockout.

After the first color is printed, remove the freezer paper and clean the colorant off with varsol. Burn off the oil if HF series is used. Then position the second piece of freezer paper (the dull side is always next to the screen) under the screen. This will block out the area where the first printing was made.

Printing Two Colors on Two Blanks

If the colors in a two-color design are overlapping, it is necessary to print each part of the design on separate blanks. One part of the design must therefore be reversed as the printing on one blank is turned up on the mold and the printed side of the other blank is turned down, thus meshing the two parts of the design. If both blanks are to be placed up on the mold, of course, do not reverse part of the design.

To reverse the design for one of the blanks, place a piece of carbon paper with the carbon side up under the paper on which the design is drawn. Trace the design and mark each part according to the color, which identifies the part of the design to be applied to each screen. If only one screen is used, trace one part of the design on the screen with pencil and proceed as for a one color design. After printing on one blank, clean the screen and squeegee with varsol. Then remove the design with water and apply the second part of the design to the screen using the reverse part of the design and repeat the process.

Paper Technique

A design may be drawn on freezer paper, which has a plastic coating on one side, then the design is cut out and the paper adhered to the underside of the screen with masking tape at each corner. The paper is the blockout. The screen is ready for printing. Figs. 124 and 125.

If a two-color design is used, stack the two parts of the paper pattern using this procedure. On top is the pattern to be traced. Place a piece of carbon paper under the pattern, then one of the pieces of freezer paper,

Fig. 124. The design is cut out of freezer paper and adhered to the underside of the screen.

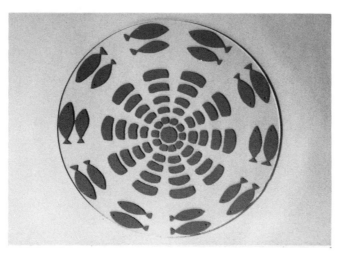

Fig. 125. The printed blank.

shiny side down, another piece of carbon paper and the other piece of freezer paper, shiny side up. Number the pieces one and two for colors to be cut out of each paper.

Before separating the pieces of paper for a two-color design, notch each end, one with a V and the other with a U. Cut a piece of thin cardboard to match these notches. Tape the designed cutout paper for the first color to the underside of the screen. Then fit the two cardboard pieces into the paper notches to match, and tape to the screen.

After the first color is printed and the screen and squeeqee are cleaned with varsol, the paper pattern for the second color will have correct placement using the cardboard notches as a guide.

Use a small pair of sharp embroidery scissors, especially for small areas, to cut out a design from freezer paper. For a one-color design, if the outline of a leaf, for example, is a part of the design, the inside will fall out. Save these pieces and adhere them to the screen with a dot of LePage's Glue in the center of the piece. (Never use Elmer's Glue on a screen.) Only a small amount is needed since the colorant will hold the paper solidly in place after the initial squeegeeing.

If a two-color design is printed, glueing the dropout pieces can best

Fig. 126. The fired piece, "Two Fishes and Five Loaves."

be done on the second color. This procedure is not practical if there are a number of dropouts. If both colors have dropouts, be sure to remove the glue from the screen with water before printing the second color.

In "Two Fishes and Five Loaves," the cutout design was taped to the underside of the screen and then a dot of glue was applied for each eye of each fish. Fig. 126.

"Sixes and Nines" is an easy design for a one-color cutout. Fig. 127.

If the paper design is to be saved, remove the paper from the screen carefully, wipe off the excess colorant with a dry paper towel, then wipe it with a paper towel moistened with varsol. After the paper is dry it may

Fig. 127. The paper design for "Sixes and Nines."

Fig. 128. "Sixes and Nines," the fired piece.

be stored and reused many times. The oil base colorant actually toughens the paper. Water, however, weakens paper, so here again water-base colorants may not be used.

To give variation to the printed blanks if they are to be laminated, sift a light application of transparent colored powdered glass on the lower blank.

Applying the Design with Glue

Iron Glue or LePage's Glue (not muscilage) may be painted directly on the screen following penciled lines traced on the silk from a planned design. In the design "Three Branches," the glue blocks out the design itself. The additional blockout needed is the plastic-coated freezer paper. The paper is cut to the size of the screen and the size of the blank is cut out of it. The paper is taped to the underside of the screen with the plastic side out, the uncoated side touching the screen. Figs. 129 to 133.

Before printing, hold the screen to the light to be sure that there are no leaks in the glued design. The screen is ready for printing.

The result of this technique gives a reverse of the application of tusche

Fig. 129. The design is applied with glue, following the penciled lines.

Fig. 130. A hole is cut from a sheet of freezer paper the size of the blank and taped to the underside of the screen.

Fig. 131. As in Fig. 119 prepare the masonite backing for proper registration of the design to the blank.

Fig. 132. The printed blank.

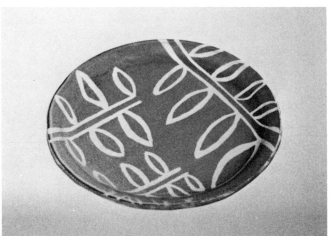

Fig. 133. "Three Branches," the fired piece.

and glue or maskoid and blockout, in that the colorant is the background with the clear glass the design.

After the screen has been cleaned with varsol, the glued design is washed off with water. If a latex emulsion, plastic-type glue, such as Elmer's Glue, gets on the silk, it will never wash off. This type of glue can be thinned with water in a liquid state but becomes waterproof when dry.

Color Plate 19. "Stitchery Hanging with Stained Glass" by Joy McFarland.

Color Plate 20. "Water Lily."

Color Plate 21. Panel using stained glass dalles and epoxy resin.

Color Plate 22. "Mobile People."

Silk Screen Kits

Silk screen kits are offered in ceramic supply catalogs. They are usually small and will accommodate blanks up to seven or eight inches square. This size screen is useful for small designs regardless of the size of the blank, that is, if only a small area of the glass is used for the design.

How To Make a Decal

Instead of printing directly on glass blanks, which has been described as a practical approach for repeating a design on a set of dessert plates, etc., decals may be made when a large number of motifs are planned. Club emblems for ashtrays or whimsical designs for window hangings can be printed in large quantities, stored away and fired on blanks at a later date.

Decals are printed on a special waxed paper on which there is a thin film of jelly on one side. This is the printing side. The design is sandwiched between two layers of varnish. The materials are available from silk screen equipment suppliers.

The procedure shown in the following pictures required only a short time for each step and can be spread over a two- or three-day period. Each coat of varnish requires four hours to dry. It would seem rather laborious to try to rush through the process. After each part of the operation, the silk screen must be cleaned with varsol.

PROCEDURE

The motif, "Gooney Bird," covers a two-inch square area. Large sheets of decal paper, 25 x 36 inches, were cut into 12-inch squares. Guide marks were made on the printing surface with a pencil for proper placement of the paper. The screen was prepared with a piece of freezer paper taped to it with the open area cut one-half inch smaller than the decal paper. This served as a blockout. Fig. 134. The first coating of varnish was silk-screened to the jelly side of the decal paper Fig.135 and 136.

Fig. 134. Decal paper is positioned for the first coating of varnish. Freezer paper with an opening one-half inch smaller than the decal paper is taped to the clean screen. The silk is stained by a former design that has no effect on the printing.

Fig. 135. The varnish is poured at the edge of the screen.

Fig. 136. The varnish is squeegeed across the screen.

Fig. 137. The varnished decal paper is positioned, using masking tape to guide accurate registration of the printing. The screen has a design on it that was applied with tusche and glue.

Fig. 138. The design is printed.

When dry the paper was cut into three-inch squares. The design, applied to the screen with tusche and glue, was printed with a Versa color to which a small amount of Thompson's HF color was added to make it more opaque. Fig. 137 and 138. Fig. 135 shows the type of printing in which the iridescence of the Versa color enhances the fired piece. Small motifs are sharper if the glaze is opaque.

When the printed design loses its sheen it may be considered dry and is ready for a top coating of varnish. The decals may be tacked onto a 12-inch square of paper held by a dab of rubber cement in the center of each square and the varnish silk-screened on sixteen motifs at a time or handled separately as shown. Fig. 139.

When the varnish is dry the finished decal is trimmed, leaving a small border just large enough to handle it when it is slipped on to the glass blank.

Submerge the decal in warm water and remove it after about 15 seconds or when it is evident that it has loosened from the backing. Slide it onto the blank as shown in Fig. 140. If an edge of the dried varnish overlaps, cut through it with a small sharp knife or razor blade and peel it off. Smears on the glass are removable with a paper towel dampened with water. Gently raise the decal and smooth it if an air bubble is trapped during the application. Unless this is done there will be a colorless hole in the motif.

Sift a very light coating of transparent clear flux or ice over the blank and fire on a mold or flat as planned. If a decal is to be laminated, prefire the blank to 500 degrees F. flat. The fired piece, "The Gooney Bird," Fig. 141.

Transfer Printing

BLOCK

Motifs and other designs may be printed on glass using a transfer method. Cut the design out of sheet cork that has a smooth surface. Sand with fine sandpaper if necessary. Adhere all of the parts of the design to a block of wood. Wet the cork thoroughly with squeegee oil and allow it to soak in before printing. Press the block against the glass. If the printing is incomplete, wash the glass and paint more oil on the cork. Sift opague powdered glass over the printing and tap off the excess. Proceed as for any design that had been applied with oil.

Do not allow the oil to get on the wood, especially if the cork is thin. If any part of the design does not print clearly at the edges, correct it after the oil is dry or after burning off the oil in a 300-degree oven as described in chapter six.

Fig. 139. The cleaned screen has a freezer paper framing taped to the screen. The cutout is one-half inch smaller than the printed squares. This is in preparation for applying the second coating of varnish. Another method of handling this step is described in the text.

Fig. 140. The trimmed decal is submerged in water for 15 seconds and then slipped onto the glass blank as the backing is pulled away.

Fig. 141. "The Gooney Bird," the fired piece.

SILK SCREEN

The technique of using dry powder on a silk screen may be called silk screen printing, although the term refers to the use of a squeegee. The method described here is considered a transfer method although the screen is involved.

The silk screen is prepared with either tusche and glue or another liquid, which is removed after the silk screen has been coated with a blockout, described in this chapter. Lay the screen on the glass blank and sift the powdered glass over it. Lift the screen carefully so as not to disturb the powder. It may be sprayed before laminating or placed on the mold without any further preparation. If it is not laminated, follow the instructions for firing the powders on the surface of the glass in chapter three.

If the design lends itself to having the powder feather out around the edges, suspend the screen about one-quarter of an inch and sift over the screen onto the glass blank.

8

Firing Schedules

Proper firing is essential when working with glass. The design on the blank may be well executed and embossed pieces intricately cut but poor firing will result in an unacceptable piece.

Before determining which schedule is applicable to a specific firing, certain factors must be taken into consideration.

Know Your Kiln

Each kiln has its own personality. Most of them have hot spots. More than a thirty degree difference, either over or under the desired temperature, will reflect in the end product.

The edges of the glass will have their original sharpness if underfired. Also, if laminated, the edges of the blanks will show the two or more pieces separately instead of becoming one piece with a single rounded edge. Unless there are large bubbles in the finished piece, underfired pieces may be refired.

The results of overfiring are numerous. If the heat is drastically excessive, the glass will become a lump in the bottom of the mold. This would happen only if the switches of the kiln were put on high and forgotten. Never stray far from the kiln when the switches are on the high position. Indications of less drastic overfiring may be recognized if there are pinpoints at the edges of the glass. Also, the edges will have a slight frosting with little grooves in them. If the shape is slightly distorted, that is, what was once a perfect circle becomes slightly ovaled, it is the result of overfiring, firing too fast, or the piece being too close to the elements.

TEST FIRE

As the kiln is being loaded, record the placement of each piece. The same type of glass and the same design technique should be used on all the pieces for these tests. When the fired pieces are removed from the kiln, label the diagram or record sheet with underfired, overfired, etc., and include the firing schedule used.

It will be a great advantage to establish the behavior of the kiln. The slightly underfired areas may be used for single blanks of double-strength glass. Use overfired areas for plate glass and for two blanks with embossed pieces. The just-right areas will take laminations without embossed pieces. The differences in the temperature needed for these glass pieces are so small that the same cone is used when a pyrometer is not available.

An excessively cool or hot spot in the kiln will most likely embrace a small area. Avoid it when firing small like pieces. Such spots do not affect a large piece that takes up most of the shelf, including the trouble spot.

The distance between shelves is ideally six inches when the pieces have depth to them. If the glass is to be slumped in a shallow mold, four-inch posts may be used. The glass on the top shelf should be at least four inches from the top of the kiln.

One adjustment that can be made when the bottom shelf produces underfired pieces is to use posts long enough so that the two lowest elements are below the shelf directly above them. Also, by raising the lid of a top-loading kiln for one-half minute near the time that the maximum desired temperature is reached, the upper part of the kiln will cool down approximately fifty degrees F.

It is better to use posts and shelves for the individual pieces than to place molds on kiln shelves that span the area of the kiln. However, this is difficult to handle in a small kiln unless very small pieces are being fired. It does contribute to an even firing.

Ventilating the Kiln

TOP-LOADING KILNS

If there are two or three peepholes in the top-loading kiln, the bottom hole should be left open and the lid raised one inch when the kiln is turned on. For a two-hole kiln, the cones are placed in front of the lower hole. The cones are placed in front of the middle hole of a three-hole kiln.

If a pyrometer is used that is not permanently installed, make a hole in the peephole plug and insert the pyrometer in it. If the kiln has two holes, leave this plug out for the first two hours while the kiln is on low and prop the lid up one inch. If the kiln has three holes, place the plug with the pyrometer in the middle hole and leave the bottom hole open. As always, the lid is propped one inch.

For one-hole kilns, the ventilation is supplied by the propping of the lid.

FRONT-LOADING KILNS

To ventilate front-loading kilns, the door is left open about one-half inch with the holes plugged for the first two or three hours with the switches on low. After this, the door is set to be only slightly ajar until the 022 cone starts to bend or the pyrometer reads 900 degrees F. When the door is closed, the same firing schedule is used for all type kilns.

Firing

Two cones are used for each firing. The first cone indicates when to close the kiln. The 022 cone is the lowest temperature indicator and bends when the temperature reaches approximately 1085 degrees F. The kiln is closed when the 022 cone starts to bend. If a pyrometer is used, the kiln is closed when the internal temperature reaches 900 degrees F.

When the second cone bends, the kiln is turned off. The number of the cone is determined by the type of glass used. Most glass requires an 015 cone. When a pyrometer is used, the kiln is turned off when 1400 to 1425 degrees F. is reached. The temperature for stained glass is approximately 1300 degrees F. Two firings for a piece use a different schedule.

FIRING FLAT

Small pieces, such as window hangings, Color Plate 14, may be fired directly on a kiln shelf on which high-fire kiln wash has been sifted. The space between the shelves may be as little as three inches. Turn the kiln on low for one hour, ventilated. Then turn to high and close the kiln when the 022 cone bends or when the pyrometer reading is 900 degrees F. Leave the switches on high until the firing is completed.

If a small enameling kiln is used, ventilate for one-half hour after turning the kiln on, then close and turn off when the edges of the glass have rounded. No cone is needed, since using the peephole or looking at the piece during the firing by opening the door slightly will reveal when the firing is completed. The total firing time for a stained glass hanging is about one and one-half hours, including the half hour when the kiln is ventilated. There should be a one-inch space between the floor of the kiln and the kiln shelf.

The schedule recommended for firing flat refers to the pieces described. If a blank or blanks are to be fired flat before a second firing on a mold, the regular firing schedule is used.

FIRING ON MOLDS

When firing pieces on molds, the slumping or bending takes place near the end of the firing period. For stained glass the contour begins at about 1000 and is completed by 1150 degrees F. Other glass, except lead crystal, starts to slump at about 1100 and takes on the shape of the mold by the time 1250 degrees F. is reached.

Regardless of the firing schedule used, all switches should be on high during the time that the contour of the glass is in the process of change. If cones are used, the interim temperatures are not known. Use peepholes or raise the lid of the top-loading kiln to determine whether the glass has settled in the mold. When this part of the firing is completed, turn the switches to low for a few minutes. Then turn them to high again and leave in this position until firing is completed.

The firing data and firing schedules presented in this chapter are the results of six years of careful record-keeping. This embraces approximately five hundred firings in two kilns. Although initially, this was done for personal use only, the records became valuable research information.

The results of the firings were recorded on the sheets with the firing schedule and revealed what schedule was best for the type work executed and what worked satisfactorily regardless of which kiln was used. Sometimes an inadvertent change in the schedule of firing turned out to be an improvement.

Most kilns used in the home are small in comparison to the ones in the studio and the classroom. The larger the kiln and the greater the number of pieces being fired, the more likely it is that a slow firing will be accomplished. A complete firing should take at least four hours.

Small kilns that are not heavy-duty kilns, that is, not well insulated, will heat up and cool down more quickly.

Reasons Behind the Firing Schedules

Raising the lid or opening the door of a kiln slightly for three minutes after firing has been completed and the kiln is turned off, reduces the maximum temperature required and will stop further softening of the glass. After that the kiln should be kept closed until it has cooled. During this period, between the temperatures of 1010 and 955 degrees F. for single- and double-strength glass made by Libby, Owens, Ford (LOF) annealing will take place if the glass is allowed to remain within the annealing range for a period of time. It is likely that most glass of this type has close to the same annealing period. See the chapter on Annealing of Glass.

The kiln should have all switches on low for two or three hours, ventilated. If the kiln is kept on low longer, it will have little effect on the firing. Most kilns will reach a temperature of between 450 and 550 degrees F. on low in two or three hours.

It is recommended to cut back the switches at certain intervals during the remainder of the firing, once they have been turned to the high position, to prevent the temperature from going up too fast. Glass heats from the outside in. The cutting back of the switches during the last two hours of firing is done to allow the inside of the glass to catch up with the outside. If the kiln heats slowly, especially large, loaded kilns, this step may prove unnecessary. It is for the craftsman to decide.

Medium speed on kilns means that half of the elements are on high and the alternating ones are off. The book that comes with a kiln will show what the position of the switches relates to in terms of the elements. The medium speed created irregular heat distribution and was used near the end of the firing only if it was necessary to compensate for temperature differences within the kiln. The test firings will indicate the need for this. When establishing the firing schedules, two pyrometers were used in each type of kiln.

If the bottom shelf of a two- or three-hole kiln produces underfired pieces, instead of keeping the switches on the high position a little longer after the cone bends or the pyrometer reaches the desired temperature, turn all switches off except the bottom one. Turn the bottom switch on medium for an additional ten or fifteen minutes. Only the lower element is on high when using the medium position for any one switch. Usually one switch controls two elements.

If the pieces placed on the top shelf of a top-loading kiln are underfired, place the top shelf further down into the kiln for subsequent firings. For a front-loading kiln, if the pieces closest to the door are underfired, place them back further when loading the kiln. These observations of the behavior of the kiln should be included in the test-firing diagrams suggested.

The firing schedules are for kilns shown in Chapter 1. Cone 015 bent but not otherwise distorted comes closest to the desired 1425 degrees

F. for single- and double-strength glass. Stained glass uses an 017 cone, which is closest to the desired 1300 degrees F. A pyrometer is the most efficient measurement of the internal temperature of a kiln. When using cones, look through a peephole or raise the lid slightly to observe the glass when near the end of the firing period. The firing is completed when the edges of the pieces are rounded and the glass has a red glow.

A Simplified Schedule

A simplified schedule may be satisfactory for some kilns. Experimenting will prove if it can be used to achieve a satisfactory firing. The pieces should be kept about one inch from the kiln wall.

1. All switches turned to low for two or three hours, ventilated.

2. Plug bottom hole, if open, after this period.

3. Turn all switches on medium for one and one-half hours, close the door or lid when 022 bends or the temperature reaches 900 F.

4. Turn switches to high until firing is completed. For single, double, and plate glass, the temperature is 1400 to 1425 degrees F. For antique (stained) glass the temperature is 1300 degrees F.

Firing Schedule

LAMINATED SINGLE- AND DOUBLE-STRENGTH GLASS
AND PLATE GLASS

All switches are on low for two or three hours with kiln ventilated as described earlier. After this period all peephole plugs are in (if any). Door or lid is closed when 022 cone bends or pyrometer reads 900 degrees F.

The temperature of the kiln at the end of the period that switches are on low is between 450 and 550 degrees F. Then follow table.

Position of Switches	Time in Minutes HD	Other	Temperature Reached
High	11	8	650 Degrees F.
Low	7	7	
High	22	12	750
Low	6	6	
High	24	15	900
Low	5	5	
High	25	16	1100
Low	4	4	
High	35	22	1300
Low	3	3	
High	until		1425 is reached

This schedule is recommended if the simplified schedule presents problems. It was developed to retard fast firing and retain even heat distribution. If any part is to be skipped over, such as leaving the kiln on high until the temperature has gone up 300 degrees F. before turning it to low, this should be done during the early part of the firing after turning the kiln on high. The time shown to reach the temperatures at the right of the table will vary with different size kilns and the size of the kiln load. However, it should be very close most of the time, since other kilns were used for tests and followed the same pattern when using this schedule.

When cooling, the heavy-duty kiln reaches 1100 degrees in about one hour, and 1010 degrees (for annealing LOF) in one hour and 35 minutes. The other kiln reaches 1010 degrees F. between 45 minutes and one hour.

SINGLE BLANKS

When firing single blanks of single- and double-strength glass, use the firing schedule for laminations but cut off the kiln at 1400 degrees F.

Firing Schedule for Antique Glass

The same schedule applies to stained glass (antique) as for single, double, and plate glass up to the time the kiln is turned to low after the temperature reaches 900 degrees F. When the kiln has been turned up after the five minute interval on low, it should be kept on high for 34 minutes for a heavy-duty kiln and for 22 minutes for the other type kiln. These are approximations. The safest schedule is to turn the kiln back to the low position when you know that the pieces have settled in the mold and leave it in that position for three minutes before completing the firing. After this three minutes, the kiln is turned up and allowed to remain on high until the pyrometer reads 1300 to 1325 or the 017 cone bends. A quick look will tell when to turn off the kiln if there is any question.

Two Firings

LAMINATED SINGLE- AND DOUBLE-STRENGTH GLASS

All of the information up to now refers to accomplishing a finished piece in one firing regardless of its individual characteristics. The recommended temperature to complete the firing for laminated pieces is based on achieving well-rounded edges.

By firing pieces flat first, the edges round earlier since there is no pull that otherwise takes place during slumping or bending on a mold.

Fire pieces flat, laminated, following the firing schedule in this chapter and turn off at 1400 degrees F. The kiln shelf on which the piece is fired must have a separating powder sifted on it. After the piece has cooled, it is refired on a mold to 1300 degrees F. The firing schedules remain the same except that the cutoff temperature is different. The fired piece is less apt to pick up separating powder on the underside when bending. Two firings prevent unwanted bubbles which would otherwise show up in some designs.

SINGLE BLANKS

Two firings are needed for a single blank of single- or double-strength glass if it is decorated on the underside and no spray equipment is available and if the design does not lend itself to the use of oil.

The opaque powdered glass is sifted on the blank and the planned design executed. The blank is fired flat on a prepared kiln shelf, the powdered side necessarily up, following the firing schedule except for the cutoff temperature. By sanding the edges of the blank before applying the colorant, the maximum temperature needed for the first firing is 1300 degrees F. The second firing, which is on the mold, uses the same firing schedule and is fired to 1300 degrees F. If the edges of the blank are not prepared, the piece will have to be fired to 1400 degrees F. in the first firing to achieve rounded edges. See Color Plate 10 "Paisley."

9

Annealing of Glass

The reason for annealing glass is to remove the internal stresses that are likely to be present. Glass that is cooled quickly from a high temperature contains internal stresses that may cause it to break spontaneously. Strained glass is known to be birefringent, or doubly refracting, and when viewed between crossed polarizers, it shows interference colors. Unstressed or annealed glass when viewed under these conditions remains dark. Thus, this method is commonly used to determine the state of annealing of a particular piece of glass.

Most glasses have an annealing range of about 100 to 200 degrees F. at some elevated temperature. When strained glass is reheated to this annealing region, the upper limit of which is slightly above the annealing point, the stresses are released in a reasonably short time. By slow cooling, the glass is annealed and shows no color pattern when viewed in polarized light.

The microstructural pattern, that is, the detailed arrangement of the atoms in the glass itself that takes place during annealing, has not been established with certainty. In the charts observed from several sources, it can be stated that the molecular pattern is more orderly in annealed glass than in glass that has not been annealed.

The coefficient of expansion of annealed glass is different from that of the same glass that has not been annealed. See Stanworth's *Physical Properties of Glass*. A bowl was made by laminating two blanks with opaque enamel powdered glass between them. The surface of the upper

127

blank was decorated with fragments of glass from the same sheet, coated with an ice. This was fired on a mold and annealed in one operation. A small circle of glass cut from the same sheet was added to further enhance the design and the bowl was refired and annealed. A fracture occurred only around the circle that had been added.

In Table X1 G-1 in Tooley's *Handbook of Glass Manufacture,* the annealing range of window glass (single strength) is from 1070 to 934 degrees F. Within this range, specific information as to the annealing range of the glass from a particular manufacturer is available on request. If the name of the manufacturer is not known, and thus the annealing range cannot be identified, the figures quoted from Tooley's *Handbook* may be considered adequate.

Stresses in the glass are relieved quickly in the upper part of the annealing range and more slowly in the lower part. The thicker and larger the glass, the longer it should remain within the annealing range. The upper end of the annealing range is the annealing point.

After firing glass pieces to 1425 degrees F., if that is the temperature to complete the firing, turn off the kiln. Raise the lid or open the door one-half inch for a few minutes to quickly reduce the temperature enough to prevent overfiring. Close the kiln and allow to cool until it reaches the annealing point. Then turn all switches to low. The temperature change will be very slight after the kiln has remained on low for one-half hour. The size and type of kiln and how full the kiln is loaded have an effect on how well the constant temperature is maintained. If, by chance, the temperature goes above the annealing range, turn off the kiln and allow it to drop back to within the range before turning to low again. However, this was not necessary when annealing in the kilns used.

In the two kilns used for the tests, the shortest amount of time for cooling to 1000 degrees F. was forty-five minutes and the longest in a heavy-duty kiln was one hour, 35 minutes. In each case, the low position of the switches kept the temperature well within the annealing range for two hours. After the kilns were cut off to cool, the temperature remained within the range for a period of time.

If the temperature had been allowed to drop below the annealing point before annealing, it would have been necessary to turn the kiln on high to return the temperature to the annealing point.

Two like pieces made from glass from the same manufacturer were tested for stress. They were seven-inch diameter laminated plates of single strength glass with transparent powdered glass sandwiched between the blanks and fired to 1425 degrees F. When the fired piece that had remained near the annealing point for fifteen minutes was observed in a polarizer, it showed that the stress was negligible and it was considered a satisfactory annealing. This was compared with the other piece with all things equal except that it was kept near (just below) the annealing point for a longer period. Little, if any, difference in the strain pattern was present. The annealing period for both pieces was extended by an additional amount of time, since the temperature of the kiln was still within the annealing range after it was turned off to cool.

It is difficult to know how much larger a piece would have to be before the amount of time that the temperature was kept within the annealing range would be ineffective. If the glass is thicker than this sample, a longer annealing period would probably be needed. If glass objects are large, the annealing period would have to be lengthened. If the glass is thicker and larger than the sample, further increase in the time would be necessary for successful annealing.

The fact that annealing is accomplished in a relatively short time makes it possible to successfully anneal small pieces, especially in a well-insulated kiln, without turning the switches to low when the temperature enters into the annealing range. By observing the pyrometer as the kiln cools, the craftsman is able to determine the amount of time the temperature remains within the annealing range. In a heavy-duty kiln, the temperature remained within the annealing range for thirty-seven minutes. LOF glass has a short range of 1010 to 955 degrees F. for single- and double-strength glass. By viewing it through a polarizer, it was evident that the annealing was successful for a nine-inch laminated piece using single-strength glass. Most laminated double-strength glass needs more time in the annealing range than the normal cooling time of the kilns used.

Annealing Without a Pyrometer

If the fired piece is very large and/or heavy, it is likely that annealing will not take place by allowing the kiln to cool normally. It can be assumed that the temperature is still above the annealing range one-half hour after the firing has been completed and the kiln has been turned off at 1425 degrees F. Turn the switches to low at this time. The low position of the switches does not provide enough heat to hold this high internal temperature constant.

The time during which the temperature is above the annealing range cannot be counted since the viscosity of the glass is too low to contribute to stress in the glass. The temperature will slowly slip into the annealing range and stay within its limits for a satisfactory annealing, if left on low for several hours.

Annealing Stained Glass

Since the coefficient of expansion of glass is changed by annealing, it can be assumed that the process can serve, in part, as a correction factor when unlike glasses are to be combined and fused together. However, annealing in itself does not make unlike glasses compatible. It will not completely obliterate all possibility of fractures.

The formulas for stained glass are necessarily different for each color, since the oxides and chemicals determine the colors and thus the differences in the coefficients of expansion. Reds, oranges, purply blues, and certain golden yellows may fracture when fused to other colors, although this is not a problem when fused to each other. There is cadmium sulfide in the formulas of these colors. Most other colors may be combined and fused without preannealing if correctly fired.

Most hand-blown antique glass has been annealed. Most colored, rolled sheet glass has been cooled quickly and is brittle (soft). This is evident when handling the two types of glass. Antique (stained) glass can be scored and severed easily when cutting long curved strips, whereas rolled glass will often fracture when you are attempting to sever these pieces.

PREANNEALING

To preanneal stained glass, fire all pieces separately in the same kiln-load before combining the parts that make up the whole to be fused. All of the glass should be from the same manufacturer.

Sift high-fire kiln wash on the kiln shelves and fire glass flat, using the stained-glass firing schedule. Since this is a first firing, with none of the components combined, it is not necessary to take the temperature beyond the annealing point. The annealing range for Blenko glass is from 1000 to 700 degrees F. As explained earlier, the annealing point is the most effective to use, that is, the highest temperature in the annealing range. In the case of this glass, the annealing point is 1000 degrees F. However, there is usually variation in the temperature throughout the kiln. To be sure that all parts of the kiln are within the annealing range, consider the upper extreme of the range to be 975 degrees F. when annealing begins.

To effectively anneal this glass, it should remain within the annealing range from two to four hours. The time period is determined by the thickness and surface size of the glass. One inch thick dalles would require the maximum time; thin blanks and pieces the minimum of two hours.

After the initial preannealing, all the components may be combined and fired either flat or on a mold, using the firing schedule for stained glass. It is unlikely that small shards of stained glass will be fused to dalles, but if they are, the maximum time for annealing is required.

Since the temperature required for fusing the combined pieces is beyond the annealing range, reannealing is necessary.

Preannealed pieces that were combined, fired, and reannealed were tested using orange and red with blue, purply blue on colorless antique glass, etc. The results were satisfactory but there was still some doubt as to the behavior of an embossed piece on a large blank of a color known to be incompatible. Deep red was considered the greatest problem.

With so much time consumed, and a sizeable amount of antique glass used, hoping that no fracture would occur, the new challenge was to find the combination that would not work.

The results are as follows: Deep rich gold antique glass fractured when fused to a soft pale blue background. One of the small pieces was a wide oval several inches long; another was smaller. Deep red, orange, and pale gold were included in the designed blank and did not fracture.

When the described pieces were viewed through a polarizer, there was evidence of stress around all of the embossed pieces on the light blue blank but not enough to cause a fracture with the exception of the gold mentioned. This deep gold did not fracture when fused to a colorless antique blank. Fractures may still occur on these samples at some future date. One piece, comprised of pieces the colors of which are considered compatible without preannealing, is eight years old and is without evidence of strain.

CONCLUSION

Blues, greens, and their variations such as turquoise may be fused with each other without preannealing. In fact, most antique glass from the same manufacturer may be combined and fused successfully. As pointed out, preannealing is necessary for certain combinations. Deep brilliant gold is compatible to red and orange without preannealing.

No two colors have exactly the same coefficient of expansion but some are close enough to be compatible when fused together. The fact that preannealing seemed to overcome some of the problems would indicate that the firing schedule for annealing has something to do with the coefficient of expansion, since the glass used had already been annealed. But it is presumed that glass is either annealed or it isn't. Perhaps the fact that the edges were smoothed in the process of pre-annealing affected the point of fusion when small pieces were combined with the background piece.

The glass used is manufactured for use in studios that are involved in making non-fired, usually leaded windows and are not concerned with fusing glass.

10

Stained Glass

About Stained Glass

Stained Glass is a term used to describe glass that has brilliant color, vibrant whether light or dark, and is most often identified with church windows. It is termed Antique Glass by those engaged in the manufacture of it. Antique glass is handblown.

Since the formulas for making antique glass are very different from that of window glass, a different firing schedule is necessary.

Fusing

If all the formulas for antique glass were available, it would be a simple matter to know which colors could be combined and fired together satisfactorily. The addition of oxides and other chemicals to the silica to obtain a wide range of colors involves carefully controlled mixtures. Differences in formulas cause differences in the coefficient of expansion. Reds and oranges and some brilliant, deep golds are compatible to each other but not to other colors. In addition to these colors, some very deep purples cause a fracture when fused to a light color. Although formulas differ necessarily to obtain different colors, most colors may be combined with each other and fired satisfactorily with the exceptions mentioned.

As explained in the chapter on annealing, preannealing before fusing may be an offsetting factor in some cases.

134

Fig. 142. Stained glass screen, approximately five feet high and six feet wide in the dining-room of a private home. Designed for viewing by both artificial and natural light. The stained glass is laminated on plate glass using a resin base adhesive. By Mariette Bevington.

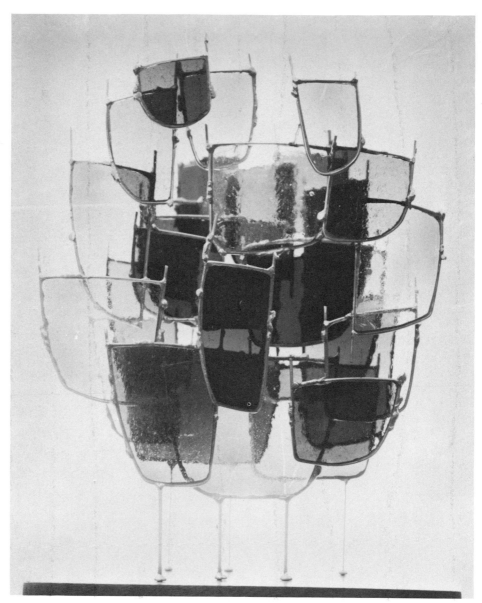

Fig. 143. "Autumn Shadows," a three dimensional stained glass construction in shades of amber, gold and violet, approximately 18 inches high. The pieces are framed in brazed brass rods, the glass is inserted with an epoxy, and the supporting framework is made of brazed brass rod. Collection of R. Leigh Glover, by Mariette Bevington.

Test firing is recommended before firing the designed piece. This can be done at the time other prepared pieces are being fired. Sift a separating powder directly on the kiln shelf and place the assembled piece on it. Remove the test piece from the cooled kiln and put it aside for a few days in order to complete the test. Strain, not immediately discernable, may be present and a fracture may show up days or even months after the pieces have been fired.

Slumped Blank With Design Embossed

Caution should be taken when fusing cutout pieces to a large blank. Avoid having the largest pieces in the center of the blank. Even distribution of the weight of the pieces will contribute to a satisfactory firing.

The position of the switches should be kept on high when the 022 cone starts to bend or, if using a pyrometer, after 900 degrees F. has been reached (see firing schedules). This procedure is recommended so that there is no chance for the glass to be caught in the process of slumping. Once the change in the contour of the glass has started, the sooner it rests on the bottom of the mold, the better. Turn the switches back to the low position for three minutes after the change in the contour has completed, then return the switches to the high position until 1300 degrees has been reached or the 017 Orton cone bends.

Uniformity in the thickness of the embossed pieces assures uniform adherence to the background. Slight overfiring is better than underfiring. An example of the even distribution of weight is shown in Color Plate 5, "Freeform."

If the pieces and the background are cut from the same sheet, there is no chance of fracture. Interesting designs may be executed although the contrast will be slight.

The Water Lily

Leaves were cut and fired on the mold shown in Fig. 144. If a bisque-fired greenware cylinder is available (a vase) it may be used for

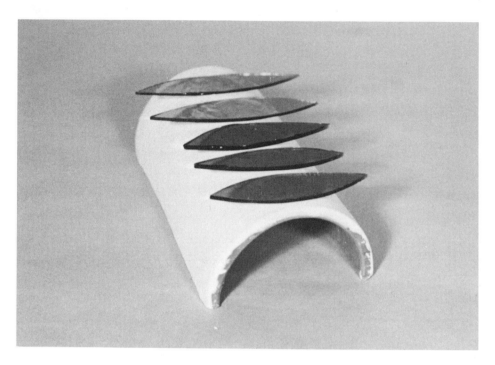

Fig. 144. Stained glass petals are balanced on a clay mold. The pieces fired on this half of a cylinder will be shiny on the outside. If they had been fired on the inside of a bowl mold, the shinier side would be inside the flower. Color Plate 20, "The Water Lily."

the mold by resting it on its side on the kiln shelf. Place a kiln post inside to prevent it from rolling. The mold shown was made by draping a rolled slab of clay over a quart bottle that was first covered with plastic wrap (see chapter on Molds). Use the firing schedule for stained glass. Turn off kiln at 1275 degrees F.

Plate glass was used for the six-inch base. The edges may be smoothed with sandpaper or a carborundum stone. Small squares of single-strength glass were adhered to the base in a circle to support the outer leaves using a two-part adhesive. (See Sources of Materials and Equipment). The small squares had to be thoroughly dry before going to the next step. Each part of this project must be allowed to dry before continuing with the procedure.

An alternative to the described base is to cut a circle of double-strength glass four inches in diameter and cut out of it a circle two and one-half inches in diameter. Score a line through the center of the total piece to remove the center. This leaves a three-quarter inch wide circle of glass to be fired on top of the six-inch base which takes the place of the glued squares. Firing rounds the edges and eliminates the necessity of sanding them. Double-strength glass is used because some of the thickness is lost in the firing. The small circle is in two pieces but will mend sufficiently in the firing.

A thick piece of stained glass may be used for the base with a small circle of the same glass on top if color is preferred.

Nip off the points of one end of the outer leaves so that an opening is left at the center of the base to allow the bottom of the blossom to set in it. It was necessary to adhere half of the leaves and allow them to dry before adding the remaining pieces. Supports were used under the leaves and a plastic jar was positioned on top of the lower ends to hold the pieces in place while drying.

The petals which make up the blossom (same mold) were stuck in styrofoam. This end is the top. The pieces were positioned so that the exposed ends, which is the bottom of the blossom, would meet with several points overlapping. A generous amount of adhesive was used on both sides of this end. More adhesive was used to bond the leaves to the blossom. Alcohol will remove excess adhesive before it is dry. The adhesive used was thoroughly dry and hard within an hour after adhering the blossom to the leaves.

Pieces Fired Flat

Separating powder is sifted on the kiln shelf and the pieces are placed directly on the powder when firing flat window hangings. Nichrome wire, which withstands high heat, is used for the hangers. The ends of the wire should be completely covered with a small piece of the same glass that is used for the background. A scant drop of

Fig. 145. Sixth grade students at the Jamestown Elementary School in Arlington, Virginia.

Scraps of stained glass were selected by the students from a supply available. Small shelves, described in the chapter on Equipment, were made by the teacher, Mrs. Rosalind Farley. The shelves were coated with a paste made of whiting and water and dusted with high-fire kiln wash using a fine sifter. The glass pieces were dotted with glue for easy handling and transporting to the kiln.

Another class used glass blanks in squares and rectangles cut from single-strength glass and decorated with scraps from the same type of glass. The scraps were colored with Versa colors to give a transluscent irridescent appearance when fired. This liquid glaze is low-fire and compatible to glass. Although it is more expensive than other glazes, very little is needed for a project. The finished pieces were framed or set in the students' window. A few students used nichrome wire hooks so that the pieces could be hung.

Elmer's glue will hold the small piece of glass, the wire, and the pieces to be fused together in place. Color Plate 14.

Non-Fired Projects

This book is concerned with glass that requires firing in a kiln. The following projects are described briefly. They do not require firing.

The Cross

The materials needed are:

Stained glass dalles, one inch thick
60/40 solder
Soldering flux
Copper foil, the thickness of thin aluminum foil
Heavy-duty soldering iron
Strong wire for reinforcing
Tool for cutting glass dalles, Fig. 7.

Copper foil was wrapped around the cut pieces of glass, overlapping the surface enough to permit the solder to curve over the outer edges of the glass. Obviously, the copper foil allows the solder to surround the glass, since it would not otherwise adhere to it.

After all of the pieces are wrapped, apply a thin coating of solder using flux to assure adherence. Line up the prepared pieces. Use a little more wire than twice the length of the finished piece. Bend the wire in half, place the bottom piece of glass in the bend, bring the wire up on both sides of the glass and twist it at the top and coat the wire and the initial layer of solder with more flux and solder. Continue adding pieces and twisting the wire and soldering. The crosspiece is prepared and attached with wire before the top part is added. The top of the cross requires a hook made of the wire that is a part of the reinforcing wire. It should not be attached separately. Form a loop with the heavy wire and embed the ends at the side of the top piece and solder in place.

The cross is hung by a chain. The sides are held in place by fish line tied to small thin hooks added at the end of each side, tacked behind the framing. The lighting is from fluorescent lights behind the frame of the twelve-inch deep alcove. Five pounds of glass and four pounds of solder were used. This was made for Mr. and Mrs. Domenic Palumbo of Alexandria, Virginia. Color Plate 17.

Stained Glass Glued Panel

The glass is cut according to the cartoon prepared from the original design. Two copies are made, one to tape to the underside of the plate glass or double-strength glass, the other to be cut up and used as the patterns for the pieces. Before separating the two copies, number each piece.

Use an adhesive that is made of a combination of resin and hardener and is especially developed to bond glass to glass. Measure a total of two teaspoons of hardener and resin in a paper cup, using the required proportions which are usually one to one. Stir quickly, paint it on the underside of the stained glass, and place the pieces on the glass backing following the cartoon.

The resin-base adhesives flow smoothly when first mixed but set up quickly. If a large amount is mixed and the adhesive starts to set, a textured appearance shows through the stained glass. Only two tablespoons of adhesive were required to adhere the pieces on the 11 × 17 inch glass panel. Color Plate 15.

If spacing is planned between the pieces of glass to allow for black grout to give a leaded appearance, cut the patterns with a double-bladed knife. Fig. 7. Special double-edged scissors are available for this purpose or the patterns can be trimmed slightly.

To prevent the grout from seeping under the glass, use enough adhesive to ooze beyond the edges when the pieces are pressed against the glass backing.

When the glass pieces will not move when forced and the adhesive is thoroughly dry, wipe the grout over the panel. After the crevises are filled, wipe the top of the glass with a damp sponge. If a small film remains, it can be wiped off after the grout is dry. White grout, used between tiles, may be blackened with a black felt-tipped marker.

If the panel is to be framed, an allowance of clear glass is needed around the stained glass pieces. If a large panel is planned, plate glass is required for the backing. For small projects, double-strength glass is sufficient. Panels may be made in sections and installed in a framing for a room divider. A panel may be made to fit a window, set in a wooden framing and screwed to the window frame.

WORKING WITH CAME

Came, calme in England, is the name of the lead strips used for stained glass windows. The layout for leading large pieces requires more detailed information than is given here. Small medallions and the pieces for the chess set in Color Plate 16 require careful cutting and positioning of the came without getting involved with waterproofing and pinning as the project proceeds.

It is necessary to stretch the came to give the leaded piece a smooth appearance and give strength to the finished piece. A six-foot length of came can stretch six inches when held in a vise at one end and pulled.

Use the minimum amount of solder needed to accomplish complete bonding. Solder one side of the project, then carefully turn and solder the other side. Clean the finished piece with a detergent solution to clean the came and remove the excess flux. Acid core solder does not require the addition of flux but those engaged in leading glass use 60/40 solid core solder and flux, either in paste or liquid form.

Came is available in many thicknesses and widths. Single-channel came is U shaped when viewed at an end and is used for the outer rim of a piece of glass, that is, no glass will abut it. Double-channel came is H shaped when viewed at the end and will accommodate a piece of glass on each side.

Mobiles require only single-channel came with loops soldered on each piece for hanging. Scraps of stained glass can make an interesting mobile. Fish line is strong and transparent, good for stringing the pieces.

Wherever pieces join, the seams should meet. The base for the chess men was leaded with single-channel came, soldered at the center of the back where it joined the upright part. This is also required when making medallions using double-channel came.

Before soldering, the came must be cleaned or the solder will not stick to it. Cleaning takes place after the came has been cut since oil from the fingers may be on the came. Scrape the joint with a knife to produce a shiny surface. Only then is there assurance that the area is clean.

If available, use 60/40 solder and liquid flux. Paste flux may be used; 50/50 solder requires more heat and does not give as smooth a finish as 60/40 solder. Because the 60/40 solder has more tin in it and thus requires less heat the chance of melting the came when leading is decreased.

Touch the solder with the tip of the heated soldering iron. The pencil-type iron may be used for light leading. Pick up a small amount of solder with the iron and place it on the joint. Do not use more solder than absolutely necessary. If too much solder is applied, carefully smooth the places with the soldering iron being careful not to melt the came.

Another method of applying the solder is to hold the solder and the iron at the joint. It is more difficult to control the solder using this method, especially if the iron gets too hot, but practice will dictate your preference of technique.

The double-channel came for the chess board was precut for all the squares in one direction, the size of each square less the space needed for the came that abutted on each end. In the other direction, the came was cut in strips the length of the chess board. As the leading proceeded, it was necessary to keep the squares firmly pushed against the already leaded part. A sheet of double-strength glass was set in the frame under the leaded board to give the needed strength. The glass used is rolled, not handblown glass to give a smooth surface.

When leaded projects are completed it is necessary to press the flanges of the came against the glass. The back of a wooden spoon is a good tool for this purpose. Projects that require waterproofing are sealed with a putty before the came is pressed.

Instructions for cutting the glass to allow for the core of the came are covered in this chapter which describes cutting glass to allow for space when using grout. The same applies to both grout and came.

DALLES

The largest stained glass window is made in sections small enough to be handled in any workroom, whether it is leaded or made with dalles and epoxy resin.

Dalles are available in a number of thicknesses. Those available in the United States are three-quarters of an inch, one inch, and one and one-quarter inches. Most of these stained glass blocks are eight inches square but several other sizes are available.

Experience in cutting dalles is needed for accurate elaborate designs. The special tool in Figure 7 is needed as well as a "pillow" for the glass to rest on when separating a scored piece. Most craftsmen engaged in working with dalles score both sides before attempting to sever the piece.

An epoxy resin has been developed to comply with the coefficient of expansion of the dalles and is recommended for outdoor and indoor use. Concrete may be used for projects planned for indoors where the temperature change is negligable.

Scraps of dalles are available through suppliers and from stained glass studios involved in the use of dalles. These are recommended for the novice. His creative ability can dictate the distribution of shapes and colors. A sheet of plate glass suspended with a light beneath it will allow the craftsman to arrange the pieces more easily.

Edges of dalles may be chipped, which will permit the light to bounce off at angles. This has the effect of the facets in a diamond. For this reason, windows made with dalles are called, "faceted stained glass windows."

Fig. 146. Decorative screen in an apartment house lobby, made with glass dalles in concrete which has a black colorant mixed in it and is set in a tubular steel frame. Since each section is small, no reinforcing was used. By Mariette Bevington.

Wherever the glass is faceted, it must be filled in with a plastic non-drying clay. The clay is removed after the epoxy resin has hardened. It is reuseable.

Epoxy resin is completely hardened in 24 hours. It must be quickly and thoroughly mixed, as it starts to set in about one-half hour. Two manufacturers have supplied the information that a single panel may be as large as three by five feet. No reinforcing is required.

PROCEDURE

Two copies of the pattern are made on paper and a number is given to each part. The same procedure is followed as for the stained glass panel that was glued. One copy of the pattern is cut up and used as a guide for cutting the dalles. The other copy is the cartoon and is attached to a piece of plywood larger than the planned slab. Freezer paper that is plastic coated on one side is a good surface for the cartoon because it releases from the poured epoxy without further treatment. Darken the lines of the cartoon on the plastic coated paper if necessary.

The paper on which the cartoon is drawn has a tendancy to draw up while the epoxy resin is maturing. To prevent this and assure a smooth surface on the underside, wet the paper before laying it on the plywood base of the frame, smooth it and allow to dry before placing the dalles.

If scraps of dalles are used to form the pattern, the freezer paper can be marked with numbers and corresponding numbers put on the glass pieces, written on masking tape attached to them.

Attach strips of wood to the plywood to form the frame of the slab to be poured. Adhere masking tape to the inside of the frame. Wipe the tape with a thin oil so that the slab will release easily. Epoxy resin will not stick to oil, grease, or dirt so it is imperitive that the dalles be thoroughly cleaned before placing them on the cartoon.

To be sure that the placement of the dalles is not disturbed, attach each piece to the cartoon with rubber cement. This will also prevent the epoxy from seeping under the dalles. Fill any faceted surfaces with plastic clay.

A thin layer of gravel may be distributed over the panel before pouring the epoxy to give a texture to the underside. Small scraps of thin stained glass or colored glass may be scattered over it. Only light colors will show up since no light is transmitted through the glass.

If pouring is done carefully, the epoxy will not get on the glass, but if it should, remove it immediately with alcohol. Epoxy sets up quickly. Use a pint size cardboard container and bend it at the edge to form a pouring spout. Since the pot life of the epoxy is short, wiping off the glass takes away from the amount of time that the mixture is pourable. Until proficiency in pouring is achieved, cover the surface of the dalles with a contact-type shelf paper that has an adhesive on one side protected by waxed paper that is pulled away before using. It is easily removed when the epoxy hardens.

Epoxy resin is available in a number of colors. The completed panel may be painted with a resin-base paint. Fine gravel or clean silica sand may be distributed over the poured slab immediately after pouring. A heavy application is needed to give a uniform coating. The excess is dusted off after the slab has hardened. If only a small amount of sand is applied, some will be lost in the epoxy and an uneven surface will result.

A Sheet of Glass is Blown

Raw materials are fed into a furnace, Fig. 147. When molten a glassblower collects a gob on the end of a blowpipe, Fig. 148. After blowing and centering the gob, additional shaping takes place, Fig. 149. The gob of white-hot glass is blown into the form of a cylinder and placed in a cylindrical, hinged mold, Fig. 150. The blowing continues after the cylinder has been placed in the mold, Fig. 151.

The cylinder of glass is removed from the mold and the glassblower begins to break it from the blowpipe, Fig. 152. The ends of the cylinder are removed, Fig. 154, and the length of the cylinder is scored with a glass cutter.

Fig. 147. Raw materials used in making glass are put into a furnace.

Fig. 148. The glass-blower collecting a gob of molten glass on the end of a blowpipe.

Fig. 149. Blower giving a little more preliminary shaping and blowing to the glass after having centered it on the pipe.

Fig. 150. The gob of white-hot glass is blown into the form of a cylinder and placed in a mold.

Fig. 151. The blowing continues after the cylinder has been placed in the hinged mold.

Fig. 152. The glassblower begins to break the cylinder from the blowpipe after it has been removed from the mold. After the separation has been made, the cylinder is placed in an oven and allowed to cool for five hours.

Fig. 153. The cylinder, cooled and ready to be trimmed.

152

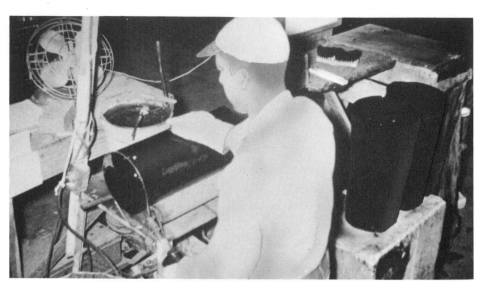

Fig. 154. Ends are removed and the cylinder is scored down the side with a glass cutter.

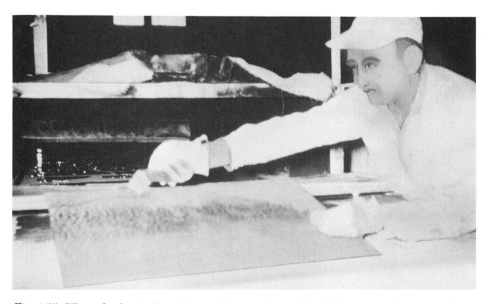

Fig. 155. The cylinder is placed in a cold oven, heated for 45 minutes, then passed into a furnace which has been heated to 1650 degrees F. The heat causes the cylinder to snap open at the scored line, and it is flattened. It is then annealed in a lehr and cooled. The workman trims the edges before it is shipped to the stained glass studio.

The cylinder is placed in a cold oven and heated for forty-five minutes. It then passes into a furnace that has been heated to 1650 degrees F. This heat causes the scored line to snap open and within three minutes a sheet is laid out. The sheet is smoothed on charcoal blocks in the furnace and rubbed down to help the flattening. It is then lifted into a furnace called a lehr and annealed before cooling. The glass is held in the annealing range of 1000 to 700 degrees F. for three hours, after which it is allowed to cool.

The hand-blown annealed sheet of antique glass is trimmed before shipping, Fig. 155.

11

Glass From Other Lands

While none of the objects shown from other countries used the techniques described in this book, most of the designs could be adapted to kiln-fired glass. In the glass designed by these contemporary artists, the artistic conception is outside the frame-work of the usual traditional approach.

It can be assumed that most of the examples of glass are lead crystal. All have been manufactured or handcrafted in commercial establishments that have facilities not available in the home.

There is a great difference between crystal and the ordinary single- and double-strength glass. A basic mixture for the so-called ordinary glass is 63 percent silica sand with soda, lime, and magnesia alumina added. Crystal is made up of 48 percent silica sand with potash, soda, lime, and red lead added. These ingredients are by no means complete. Other materials are used in small quantities. Many formulas are listed at the Corning Museum of Glass at Corning, New York, each identified as to its particular use.

The presence of lead in crystal makes the glass easier to cut, engrave, and polish. It softens at a lower temperature than ordinary glass. Lead gives brilliance to the glass and, with the addition of metal oxides to give it color, many imitation jewels are made.

In seeking out glass from other lands the emphasis was on the end product rather than the process used. That is to say, the pieces shown were chosen for the design itself rather than the technique.

154

Fig. 156. Exhibition of Czechoslovakian glass in Moscow 1959.

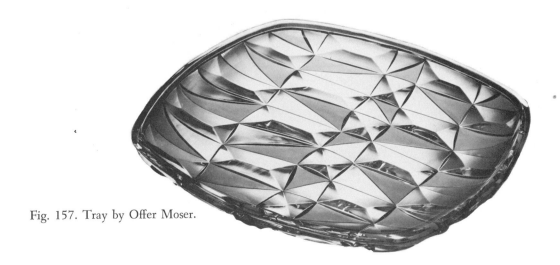

Fig. 157. Tray by Offer Moser.

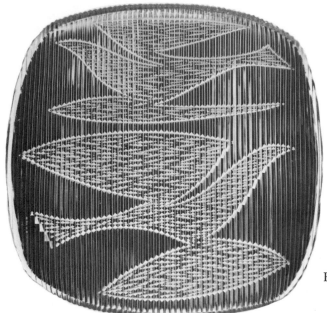

Fig. 158. Tray.

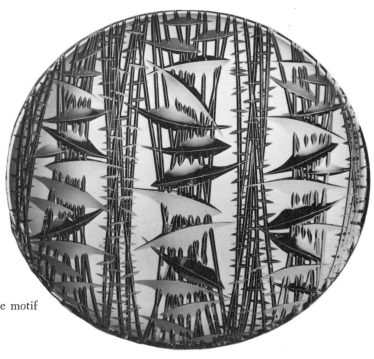

Fig. 159. Vegetable motif
by Josef Svarc.

There is great emphasis on design today. It is for the craftsman to ponder when working with glass. Being different for the sake of being different doesn't contribute to a better design. Too often the craftsman is carried away by the idea of being unique, although sometimes it does work.

On this subject there is the following comment from *Bohemia Crystal,* Prague: "The dynamic interior decoration in a modern home allows the application of new artistic trends in an unconventional creative way.

"When considering glass as a decorative accessory in the modern interior, there are a number of answers to this theme all justified in their way and therefore relatively true. This is a problem that has no definite or charactertistic norm, for everyone has a right to create in his home an environment according to his own idea and taste, with furnishings and accessories in which he himself sees the perfect expression of practical function and aesthetic appeal."

Dr. G. M. J. Heule, Managing Director of the United Glass Works in the Netherlands, said in his speech on the occasion of the opening of the Glass Design Center at Leerdam:

"The creative urge that craftsmen and artists have in common, together with the characteristic property of science that it is accessible to all, is of great importance for progress . . . .

"We believe that in the hard world of today there are signs that indicate that in the society of tomorrow "homo ludens," or man at play, will perform an important role, not as an individual, but as a socially structured person. It seems that this hard world of today has mainly been shaped by the interplay between "homo sapiens" or thinking man, and "homo economicus," whom I would call in this context competitive man.

"Looking to the future, I believe that the element of play as such will increasingly form part of the daily requirements of the new man, and will no longer just constitute an independent pattern of recreation or throwing off the cares of earning one's daily bread.

"The constant rise in the standard of living and the increase in leisure time are not foreign to this. The desire and the need of everyone to surround himself with good and pleasant things, in order to intensify the 'living climate' in the aesthetic sense, are rapidly increasing. This applies both to articles of use and to objects of a non-functional character that constitute our environment . . . .

"In point of fact, handcrafts will finally give satisfaction if people realize the value of diversity and seek newer truths and forms. . . ."

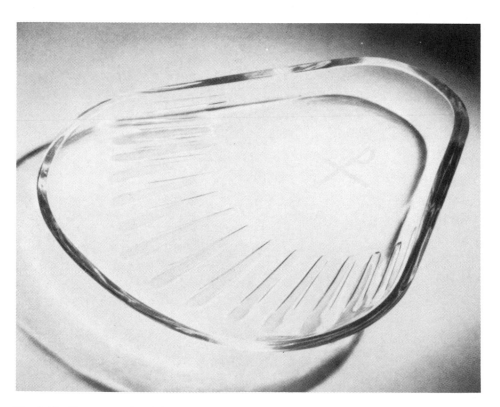

Fig. 160. Christening bowl by Arttu Brummer.

Fig. 161. Plates by Temo Sarpaneva.

Fig. 162. Fish plate by Gunnel Nyman.

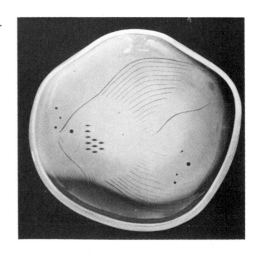

Fig. 163. One of the walls at the Royal Leerdam Glass Works. Green bottles are set in poured concrete, giving a soft green light inside the entrance. The bottles are set in separate blocks.

Fig. 164. Window using a new process.

Fig. 165. Engraved vase.

Fig. 166. Engraved bowl.

Fig. 167. Head—A statuette executed on the basis of a new process by designer W. Heesen in clear crystal. Height fourteen inches.

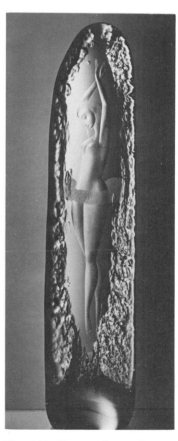

Fig. 168. Engraved crystal.

Fig. 169. Bowl of the "Ravenna" technique. Color is inlaid in the middle of the crystal in green and blue. Designed by Sven Palmgrist for Orrefors Glasbruk.

Fig. 170. Bowl designed by Gunnar Cyren for Orrefors Glasbruk.

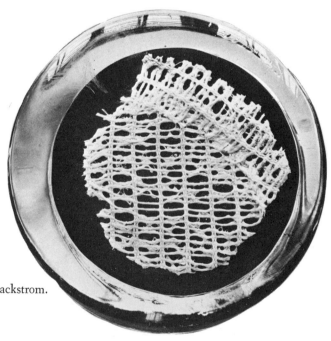

Fig. 171. "Popglas" designed by Monica Backstrom.

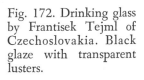

Fig. 172. Drinking glass by Frantisek Tejml of Czechoslovakia. Black glaze with transparent lusters.

Fig. 173. Turnaline by Nanny Still of Finland.

Diagrams

The diagrams on the following pages are actual size portions of circles that will be helpful to the craftsman when laying out designs by completing the diagrams on a sketch pad. Use tracing paper over the largest part of the diagram and move it frequently for accuracy. After the diagram has been transferred to the pad, go over the lines with a felt pen that has a fine point. In addition to using the diagrams for drawn designs to be repeated around a circle, they will also serve as a guide when placing small pieces of glass to be laminated or embossed.

Diagram 1 shows the layout used for Color Plate 1 and also dissects a circle in eight equal parts. The diameter of the circle is 12⅛ inches, which is what is needed to execute the design of the scallops on a 12-inch blank.

Diagram 2 has 32 curved lines embracing a 15-inch diameter circle at its largest point. A single curved line has been drawn to the center of the circle to emphasize the pivot point. Sgraffitoed lines should not go within the smallest circle if using all of the curved lines. If this diagram is used for projects involving only 16 of the 32 lines, it will prove helpful to mark the lines, 1, 2, 1, 2, etc., so as to follow only the alternating curves. In Color Plate 2, alternate sgraffitoed lines stopped at a circle larger than the innermost one to effect the pattern. When drawing this diagram use a cardboard template cut to the size of the largest curve.

Since an uneven number of repeats of a design is often very desirable, diagrams 3 and 4 are offered here as guides for dividing several circles into uneven segments.

166

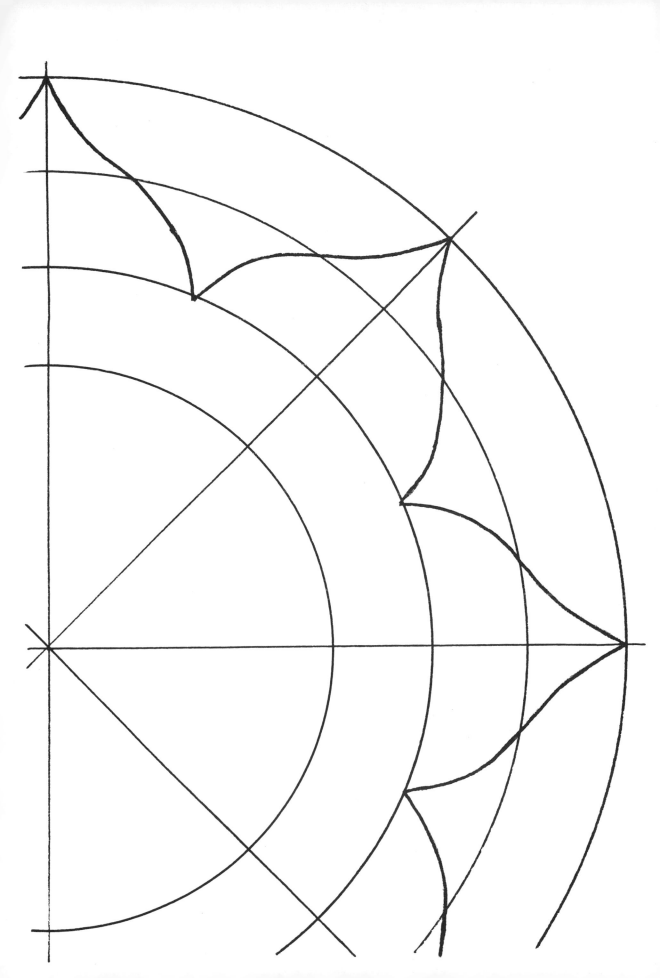

15 INCH
DIAMETER

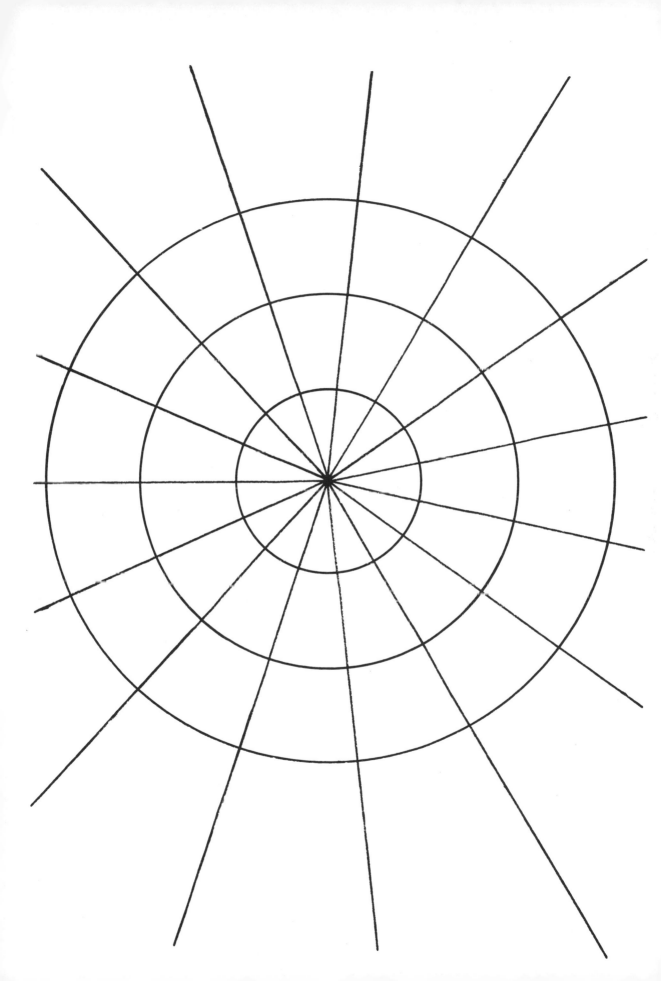

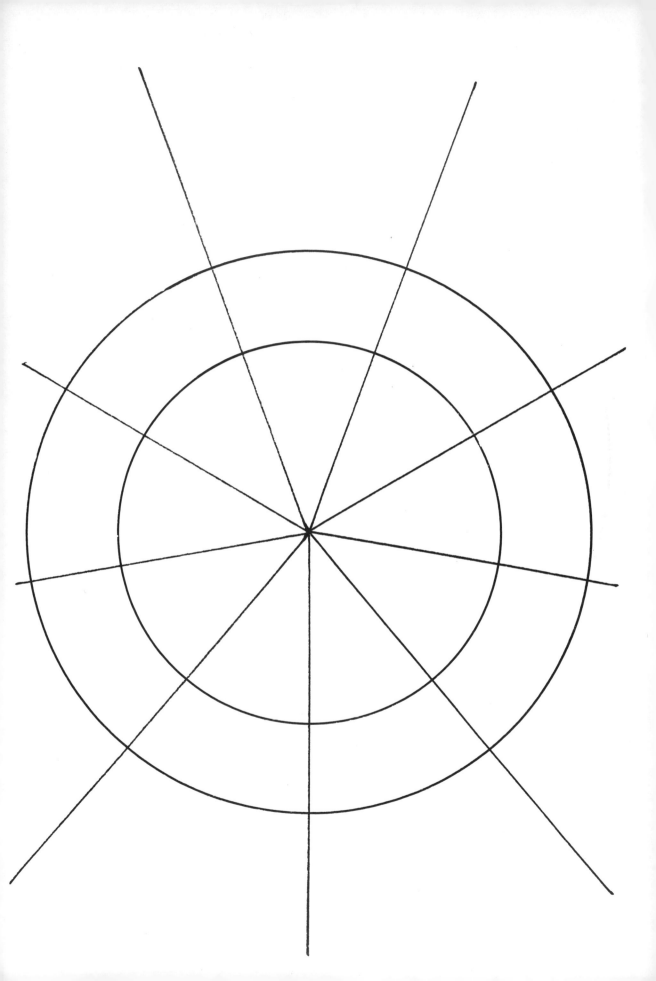

Glossary

Annealing Point: The temperature at which internal stress in glass is relieved. It corresponds to the upper end of the annealing range.

Annealing Range: The temperature span that glass is held at to allow change to take place. The effects include the removal of stress, induced softness, refined structure and altered physical properties. The upper end in the annealing range is the annealing point. The lower end within the range, and least effective in annealing, is the strain point.

Birefringent: This means "doubly refracting." The technical definition describes birefringent as: "The property of having more than one refractive index relative to the direction of the traversing light."
Glass that has undergone internal strains will exhibit double refractions. These strains are relieved by annealing when compatible glasses are combined and fired beyond the annealing point. Birefringent or unannealed glass is easily broken.

Bisque Ware: Greenware that has been fired after it is allowed to dry without the addition of a glaze. It may be used as a mold for glass providing it has other required characteristics.

Blank: Any piece of glass that has been cut into the size and shape desired for the total project. It does not refer to small pieces of glass used for decorating.

Came: Lead strips used with glass, usually stained glass, and serving as a binder. Stained glass windows, mobiles, and medallions may be made with came. There are single-channel and double-channel cames. The double-channel is the more common. When viewing it from the end, an H is evident and indicates the two channels that the glass fits into on each side. Single channel is shapped like a U when viewed from the end and is used to frame the outside of hanging ornaments or anyplace where no glass is to be added on one side. Both types of came come in six-foot lengths. They must be stretched or pulled before using (see text).

Carborundum Stone: Silicon carbide, an abrasive. Also called a whetstone. Available in round or rectangular shapes. It is used under running water to remove pinpoints that might result on the edges of fired glass. It is also used under running water to smooth irregular edges of glass before firing. If used after firing, frosted marks result.

Cartoon: The design translated onto heavy tracing paper or other paper that provides the layout for the pieces of glass planned for a stained glass window or other objects involving a number of pieces of glass cut according to a pattern.

Coefficient of Expansion: For a solid, this is the change in volume per unit volume per degree Centigrade. This is the technical description of the coefficient of expansion. From this, it is understandable that since change in glass takes place when expanding and contracting, compatibility is necessary so that the parts that make up the whole are going through this change at the same time.

Crucible: Pot in which glass formulas are heated to a molten or softened stage. It is used for mixing flux and other materials and heated to a high temperature when making enamels.

Dalles-de-verre: Commonly known as "dalle" or "dalles." The literal translation of these thick stained glass blocks is "paving stones of glass." Sizes are available from 8 × 8 inches to 12 × 12 inches and dalles are from ¾ to 1¼ inches thick. Special cutting tools are required. Usually chips·are tapped off the surface of the shaped piece to form facets. It is often referred to as "faceted glass" for this reason.

Embossing: Small pieces of glass are adhered to the surface of a blank of glass by firing.

Enamels: Basically enamel is powdered glass, either transparent or opaque, to give color and design to a glass blank. It is the same material that is used on metal. Oxides are added to flux, which is clear glass, to give it color. Certain combinations of materials are used for specific reasons. Lead, potash, and soda in controlled quantities are added for brilliance. Borax and soda or potash are used in determining the coefficient of expansion of the enamel. The depth of color is controlled by the amount of oxide that is added to the frit or flux. By the addition of tin oxide transparent enamels are changed to opaque.

Engraver: An electric tool that has a wheel or sharp point to scratch into the surface of glass.

Firebrick: A soft porous brick that will withstand high heat. It may be carved into to make small molds for glass. It is used on inside walls of kilns.

Flange: The part of lead came that stained glass is set into.

Flash Glass: Rolled glass to which a colorant has been applied on its surface and heated. It has a different coefficient of expansion than most stained glass although the surface has the same appearance. It can be identified as different from antique or stained glass by observing the side edge. When cutting flashed glass, score on the uncolored side. It should not be fused to antique glass.

Flux: Colorless powdered glass.

Frit: Colorless powdered glass that varies in formula from flux.

Fuse: Glasses combined and heated to a temperature that softens the glass enough to be unified in the process.

Glaze: A glass in liquid or powder form used for coating and decorating.

Greenware: A mixture of clay, water, and a suspending agent poured into a plaster mold, allowed to set, then removed and dried.

Ice: An enamel adjusted in formula for use on a glass surface without chipping off when fired. It is closer to being transparent than opalescent.

Jewel: Small pieces of colored glass that have been fired or embossed on glass blanks for decoration.

Lamination: When two or more blanks of glass are combined and fused in firing to become a single piece.

Marver: A flat surface on which to roll softened glass when in the process of blowing.

Mica: A mineral. When scattered on a glass blank to be laminated, little bubbles will result when fired.

Mold: Shaped materials that will withstand heat beyond the maximum temperature required to fire the glass that rests on it. Molds may be made of a variety of types of clay. Steel molds are used by craftsmen who are able to control firing.

Patching Cement: A material used to patch the firebrick wall of a kiln. It may also be used to correct the bottom of a mold for glass that requires flattening. This cement comes in fine and coarse grain. The fine grain is used to correct molds.

Pinpoints: Points that appear on the fired edges of glass objects resulting from firing too fast or from an insufficient amount of separating powder used on the mold.

Pot Life: The amount of time that combined ingredients are usable. Example: A two-part adhesive once mixed will start to harden after twelve minutes. It is not usable after that time. Thus the pot life of the adhesive is twelve minutes.

Pyrometer: An instrument that registers the temperature of the inside of a kiln on a meter. The thermocouple of the pyrometer is the part that is exposed to the heat in the kiln and is either built into the kiln or inserted in a hole made in a peephole plug.

Sagging: Also referred to as "slumping" or "bending." The act of glass taking on the contour of the mold on which it rests through the application of heat.

Score: Scratching the surface of glass, which when tapped, pressed, or snapped will separate at the score. The scoring and then severing are sometimes referred to as cutting glass. The act of scoring and severing relieves the stress in glass at the point of scoring causing the glass to snap apart.

Separating Powder: Also referred to as a parting agent. Powders either sifted on molds or made into a paste by mixing with water and applied with a brush or spray to prevent glass from sticking to the surface on which the glass is fired.

Sgraffito: The Italian word for "scratch." The act of scratching a design into a glaze or enamel, either dry powder or applied to glass while wet. A design may be scratched into damp clay before it is bisque fired when used as a mold for glass.

Silk Screen Silk: The material attached to a frame used for silk screen printing. It is not necessarily made of silk, but is a strong material that may be reused many times.

Slip: Clay mixed with water with other materials added depending on what it is to be used for.

Sodium Silicate: A liquid glass also referred to as "water glass." Its use is described in the chapter on equipment.

Strain Point: The lower limit of the annealing range that is the temperature from which a piece of glass can be quickly cooled without introducing permanent strain.

Strength of Glass: Refers to the thickness of glass.

Stress: Tension or compression within glass particularly due to incomplete annealing, temperature gradient, or incompatibility of mixed glasses.

Tempered Glass: A treatment given to plate glass as it is in the process of cooling. When the glass reaches 1200 degrees F. it is held at this temperature while 110 degree F. air is blown on the surface. The surface hardens quickly. As the cooling continues the inner part of the glass wants to expand but the outer surface prevents it. Glass cannot be cut after tempering. Attempting to do so will cause the glass to break up into tiny pieces.

Tesserae: Small pieces of glass that usually refer to squares.

Tusche: Liquid used to apply a design to a silk screen. It is used in combination with a blockout of either water-base glue or other water-base materials manufactured for that purpose. Solvent for tusche—varsol.

Underglaze: Used to decorate glass. Unless it is topped with a flux, it will have a rough texture on the surface of the blank.

Varsol: Cleaner for silk screen. Mineral spirits may be used.

Wedging Clay: The act of kneading clay to remove any air trapped in it. Any bubbles that remain in the clay will explode in the firing.

Wet Belt: A belt available in several grits, used wet on a motor driven piece of machinery to smooth the edges of glass before firing. If used after firing a slight frosting will be evident. A very fine grit belt may be used to smooth opaque powdered glass that has been fired on the underside of a glass blank, but this is a delicate operation.

Whiting: Calcium carbonate. A separating powder used in paste form. It is mixed with water and painted on the inside of a mold or on a kiln shelf. To achieve a good surface on the underside of a fired piece, in addition to the application of whiting sift high-fire kiln wash on the mold or shelf before each firing.

Wire Cloth: Metal cloth that comes in many different meshes and is actually a screening material. It is used to make sifters for applying separating powder and powdered glass.

Bibliography

Handbook of Glass Manufacture. F. V. Tooley, Ed. Ogden Publishing Company, 1953. Section XI, Annealing and Tempering.

Glass: The Miracle Maker. C. J. Phillips. Pitman Publishing Corporation, 1941. Chapter 10, Finishing Annealing, Decoration and Inspection.

Physical Properties of Glass. J. E. Stanworth. Oxford University Press, 1950.

Properties of Glass. George W. Morey. Reinhold Publishing Company, Revised Edition, 1958.

Hackh's Chemical Dictionary, McGraw-Hill Publishing Company, Third Edition.

Sources of Materials and Supplies

Manufacturer of Kiln

Cress Manufacturing Co.
1718 Gloradora Ave.
South El Monte, Cal. 91016
(Switches have infinite speed.)

L and L Manufacturing Co.
P. O. Box 348
Twin Oaks, Pa. 19016

Paragon Industries, Inc.
Box 10133
Dallas, Texas 75207

American Art Clay Co.
4717 West 16th Street
Indianapolis, Ind. 46222

Arco Kilns
4132 No. Tamiami Trail
Sarasota, Florida 33580
(Stacked rings to adjust size as needed.)

Enamels and other Colorants

American Art Clay Co. (Amaco)
4717 West 16th Street
Indianapolis, Ind. 46222
(Frit No. 3396, oxides, stains, glazes, enamels, Versa Colors for painting and silk screen printing, sprayer shown in Fig. 8.)

Arts and Crafts Colony
4132 No. Tamiami Trail
Sarasota, Florida 33580
(Enamels, glass glazes and stains, molds, good mold coating.)

Kay Kinney Contour Glass
(manufacturer and distributor)
725 Laguna Canyon Road
Laguna Beach, Calif. 92651
(Molds, glass glazes and stains, good mold coating.)

Thomas C. Thompson Co.
1539 Old Deerfield Road
Highland Park, Ill. 60035
(Enamels, ices, nichrome wire, fluxes, used in this book.)

Stained Glass

Advance Glass Company
Newark, Ohio 43055
(Rolled cathedral, seedy, variegated.)

Blenko Glass Company
Milton, West Virginia 25541
(Blown glass, in sheets and pieces, dalles; visitor's center tours.)

Charles J. Connick Associates
9 Harcourt Street
Boston, Mass. 02116
(Glass and copper foil sheets used in color plate 13.)

S. A. Bendheim Co., Inc.
122 Hudson Street
New York, N. Y. 10013
(Most types of colored and stained glass, foreign and domestic.)

Glass and Equipment for Leaded Projects

The Stained Glass Club
482 Tappan Road
Northvale, N. J. 07647
(Equipment and glass for Tiffany lamps and other projects.)

Whittemore-Durgin Glass Co.
Box 2065
Hanover, Mass. 02339
(Large supply of patterns for leaded projects incl. Tiffany lamps, related glass and tools.)

Glass Cutters

The Fletcher-Terry Co.
Spring Lane
Farmington, Conn. 06032
(All types of glass cutters, circle cutter in Fig. 6.)

Falls Church Glass Company
7728 Lee Highway
Falls Church, Va. 22042
(Excellent glass cutter shown in Fig. 40.)

Epoxy Resins for Dalles

Benesco
40 North Rock Hill Road
St. Louis, Mo. 63119

H and M Plastics Corp.
129 S. Second Street
Philadelphia, Pa. 19106

Silk Screen Equipment

Naz-Dar Silk Screen Equipment
1087 N. North Branch
Chicago, Ill. 60622
(Silk screen supplies for decals, except glazes)

Martin Supply Company
619 West Franklin Street
Baltimore, Md. 21201
(Eastern rep. for Naz-Dar)

Miscellaneous

Somma and Maca
5501 West Ogden Ave.
Chicago, Ill. 60650
(Bits for boring holes in glass, wet belts, wide-nosed pliers.)

Armstrong Acoustical Ceramic
Fireproof Insulation Sheets,
available from local building
material distributors; Trade-
name: Ceramaguard, used
on page 140 for shelves.

White Metal and Rolling Corp.
80-84 Moultrie Street
Brooklyn, N. Y. 11222
(All sizes came and
solder, came in minimum
100 lb. lots.)

Adhesive for Bonding Glass
to Glass
Duro E-Pox-E, a two-part
epoxy which dries clear.
Check package to choose
one which withstands heat
up to 200 degrees F. Available in hardware stores.

L. Reusche and Company
2-6 Lister Avenue
Newark, New Jersey 07105
(Low temperature glass
colors including lusters.)

Index

Adhesives
   Elmer's glue, 72
   for bonding glass to glass, 142
Agar, 24
Annealing
   other than stained glass, 127-130
   period, 129-131
   point, 128
   preannealing stained glass, 131
   range, 129-131
   stained glass, 130
   without a pyrometer, 130
Antique glass; *see* Stained glass
Assembly for laminations, 65

Baking soda, 77
Bartelmes, Bette, Color plate 16
Beaman, Richard B., Color plate 12
Bending, 1
Bevington, Mariette, 135, 136, 146
Bisque-fired greenware, 28, 29
Blanks
   double-strength, 2
   irregular shapes, 3
   laminated, 51, 54-63, 66-71, 74-82
   limitations of sizes, 2
   plate glass, 2
   single-strength, 2

Blenko Glass Company, 148-153
Blockouts for printing, 97
Blowing sheets of glass, 148-153
Bohemia Crystal, 155-157, 165
Bonding glass to glass, 142
Bottom of mold designs, 34-37
Brushes, Japanese, 10
Bubbles
   double, 77-79
   random, 77, 80
   single, 73-76
   unplanned, 81, 82
   unwanted, 64
Buescher, John D., Color plate 15

Calibration, 9
Came, 12
   double channel, 143, 144
   single channel, 143
Carborundum stone, 48
Cartoon, 142, 147
Chess set, Color plate 16
Chianti bottle, 34
Chips of bottle glass, 50
Coefficients of expansion, 127, 130, 133
Color samples, 20, 21
Colorants
   ceramic glazes, 14

Colorants, *continued*
  glass glazes, 14
  powdered glass, 14
    high-fire, 16
    ices, 16, 64
      opalescent enamels, 16
      opaque enamels, 15
      transparent enamels, 16, 64
Compatibility of glasses, 51, 53, 130
Cones
  behavior of, 9
  use of two cones, 119
Copper foil for stained glass, 141
  The Cross, Color plate 17
  The Gizmo, Color plate 13
Cutters, glass
  circle, 11, 46
  lubricant for, 38
  straight line, 12, 39
Cutting glass
  circles, 46-48
  irregular shapes, 42-45
  straight lines, 39-41, 49
Cutting knives, 12
Czechoslovakian glass, 155-157, 165

Dalles
  clay used in facets, 147
  cutting, 145
  epoxy resin for, 145, 146, 148
  faceting, 145
  scraps, 145, 147
  slab using dalles, Color plate 21
Decals
  printing, 111-114
  transferring to glass, 111, 114, 115
Decorating wheel, 11
Designing with separator, 37
Double-bladed knife, 12, 142
Double bubbles, 78, 79

Double-strength glass, 2

Electric sprayer, 12
Elmer's glue, 72
Embossed designs, 51, Color plates 1, 5,
  6, 9
  ices, 16
  opaque, 15
Embossed panes, 90
Embossing on underside of glass, 85-87
Enamels; *see* Colorants
Engraver, 11
Epoxy resin for dalles, 145, 147, 148
  frame for slab, 147

Farley, Rosalind, 140
Fiberglass threads, 22
Finnish glass, 158, 159, 165
Firebrick
  molds, 33-35
  posts, 8
Firing glass
  cool and hot spots in kiln, 118
  flat, 8, 120
  on molds, 120
  overfiring, 118
  test firing, 118
  underfiring, 118
Firing schedules, 27, 117-126
  antique glass (stained glass), 125
  one firing
    laminated, 123, 124
    single blanks, 124
  tables for, 123, 124
  two firings, 125
    laminated, 125
    single blanks, 126
Flange, 145
Flux
  clear glass, 25, 72

Flux, *continued*
    formula for, 25
    soldering, 143, 144
Freezer paper, 105, 107
Frits, 18
Frosted plate glass, 18
Fused glass mural, Color plate 12

Glass blanks; *see* Blanks
Glass chips, 50
Glass cutters
    circle, 11, 46
    lubricant for, 38
    straight, 12, 39
Glazes; *see* Colorants
Grease pencil, 11
Greenware
    bisque-fired molds, 28, 29
    pouring, 27
Grout for stained glass, 145
Gum arabic, 24

Hammer for dalles, 12
Heaton, Maurice, 1
Higgins, Frances and Michael, Color
       plates, 3, 6, 11

Ices; *see* Colorants
Internal stresses, 127
Irregular shapes
    cutting, 42-45
    fired piece, Color plate 10

Jamestown Elementary School, 140
Japanese brushes, 10

Kilns
    ceramic
        front loading, 4
        top loading, 4-6

Kilns, *continued*
    enameling, 5, 7
Kiln posts, 8
Kiln shelves, 6-8

Lamination
    one color, 54
    two colors, 55-63
    using three blanks, 88
Leading glass, 143
Lehr, 153

McCutchen, Earl, 18-20, 23, 52
McFarland, Joy, Color plate 19
Microstructural pattern, 127
Molds
    bisque-fired greenware, 28, 29
    carved firebrick, 34
    clay, 30-32
    design on the underside, 35-37
    from wax models, 30-32
    holes in, 29
    manufactured, 27
    pinchpot, 31-33
    separators for, 36

Netherlands glass, 157, 160-162
Nichrome wire, 140

Oil, squeegee
    burning off, 64
    painting with, 53-65, 74-82
    spattering, 89, 91, Color plate 7

Palumbo, Mr. and Mrs. Domenic, 142
Panels
    glued, 135, Color plate 15
    using dalles, 146, Color plate 21
Paper designs for silk screen, 105, 107
Parting agents; *see* Separating materials

Pinchpot molds, 31, 33
Pinpoints, 117
Plate glass
  embossed design, 81-83
  frosted, 18, 89
  tinted, 91
Preannealing stained glass, 131, 132
Printing
  block, 114
  decal, 111, 114
  dry application with silk screen, 116
  see also screen printing
Pyrometer, 5
  calibration of, 9
Pyrometric cones, 9, 119

Random bubbles, 80
Resin base adhesive, 142
Rough edges, 48
Royal Leerdam Glass Works, 157,
  160-162

Sagging, 1
Schedules for firing, 27, 117-126
Scoring, 38-46
Scrubber sponge, 11
Separating materials
  high-fire kiln wash, 8
  mold-coat, 35
  pastes, 35
  whiting, 8
Sgraffito
  dry powder, 65-71
  sprayed powder, 24
  tools, 11
Sifters
  how to make, 9, 10
  purchased, 9, 10
  screening for, 9, 10

Silk screen printing
  decals, 111-115
  designing with glue, 108-110
  designing with tusche, 96
  fired prints, 107, 108, 110, Color
    plate 8
  materials for, 93
    blockout, 96-98
    cleaner for screen, 103
    colorants, 100-102
    silk screen silk, 94
  paper technique, 105, 107
  preparation for, 99
  two color print, 103, 104, 107
Single bubbles, 74-76
Single-strength glass, 2
Slip, 27
Slip trailing, 19, 20, 26
Slumping, 1
Solder
  acid core, 10
  solid core, 10
Soldering flux, 10, 12
Soldering irons, 12
Sprayer, 12
Spraying over powder, 24
Squeegee, 93
Squeegee oil
  designing with brush, 53-65
  spattering, 89, 91, Color plate 7
Stained glass, 134
  embossed designs, 137
  fired flat, 139, Color plate 14
  fusing, 134
  non-fired projects, 141-148, Color
    plates 15, 16, 17, 21
Stitchery and glass, Color plate 19
Straight glass cutter, 12
Strain pattern, 129
Strained glass, 127

Strengths of glass; *see* Blanks
Stresses, 127-129
Swedish glass, Orrefors, 163, 164

Tesserae, Color plate 18
Thermocouple, 8, 9
Tinted plate glass, 91
Top-loading kiln, 5, 6
Transfer printing, 114, 116
Tusche, 96

Unplanned bubbles, 81, 82
Unstressed glass, 127

Varnish for decals, 111

Varsol, 106, 107
Ventilating the kiln, 5, 119
Versa colors, 101

Walters, Ruth, Color plate 18
Water lily, 138
Wax model for mold, 31
Wedging clay, 30
Wet belt, 48
Whiting, 8
Wide-nosed pliers, 10
Wire
    nichrome, 140
    cloth, 9, 10

Harriette Anderson

Mrs. Anderson's initial effort as a creative craftsman was as a textile designer. Three years of instruction under Mrs. Lyn Egbert at the Design Studio in Washington, D.C., resulted in having many of her designs sold to the trade in New York. Her fabrics have been shown at the Corcoran Gallery of Art and the Smithsonian Institution in Washington.

Later, Mrs. Anderson studied ceramics under Alexander Giampietro at Catholic University and this introduced her to the use of the kiln. Then, in 1961, she took a summer course in glass under Maurice Heaton at the Rochester Institute of Technology, in a program sponsored by the American Crafts Council. Without being aware of it at the time, she had printed her last fabric and made her last pot. Not enough had been written, and much was to be learned, about glass. The results of her successful experiments and the knowledge gained through research were carefully recorded, becoming a helpful reference for her book, although initially it was not her intention to write about them. It was her participation in the Waterford, Virginia, Fair, which attracts many thousands yearly, which inspired her to write this book, rather than comply with many requests to teach courses in kiln-fired glass.

Glass objects executed by Mrs. Anderson have been accepted in many juried shows, including those of the North Carolina Museum of Art in Raleigh, the Virginia Museum of Fine Arts in Richmond, and the Norfolk Museum of Arts and Sciences in Norfolk, Virginia, where she was given the First Award in Glass. Mrs. Anderson has also had four shows of her own in northern Virginia galleries.

Harriette Anderson has been a member of the art circles in her area for many years. She is past president of the McLean Art Club, a member of the Kiln Club of Washington, D.C., and a member of the board of the Emerson Gallery in McLean, Virginia, where she lives with her husband and son, John. Her married son, David III, resides with his family in Falls Church, Virginia.